OneTrackMinds

ONETRACKMINDS

True stories about life-changing songs

Edited by Kristian Brodie and Adam Shakinovsky

unbound

First published in 2022

Unbound
Level 1, Devonshire House, One Mayfair Place, London W1J 8AJ
www.unbound.com
All rights reserved

Text design by PDQ Digital Media Solutions Ltd.

A CIP record for this book is available from the British Library

ISBN 978-1-80018-100-7 (paperback)
ISBN 978-1-80018-101-4 (ebook)

Printed in Great Britain by Clays Ltd, Elcograf S.p.A.

1 3 5 7 9 8 6 4 2

With special thanks to

Dave Miller
Haresh Patel
Louis Shakinovsky
Amar Singh

In aid of

SAMARITANS

All author proceeds will be donated to Samaritans. A
registered charity.

Contents

Part 4 – Believing

Foreword

By Deborah Frances-White

A song, like a scent, can bring back a lost loved one, a wild romance or your whole adolescence. If you put a song away at the close of a school year, the last lap of a road trip or the end of a relationship, someday, when you rub that magic lamp in the future, out will come the musical genie. There it is, haunting and magical, right along with the dropped guitar jangle of 'A Hard Day's Night', the erotic 'wah, wah, wah' of 'Let's Get It On' or the hopeful opening arpeggio of 'Mr Brightside' – the feel of the first day of secondary school, the image of sunset at the last gas station before New Orleans, or the memory of a lover's hand in your hair under the stars at Glastonbury.

The genius of *OneTrackMinds*, the live show, is that a track unlocks a memory which releases a story – and that story tumbles from the speaker with the hues and shadows the tune has conjured in the speaker's mind. You might have come to the show because you're a fan of a certain comedian, actor or broadcaster, but the game of sharing a love for a certain song, shanty or sonata allows that artist to reveal far more than you'd see in the average interview, even if the interviewer is excellent. The melody can find recesses of that person's mind the best FBI interrogator couldn't reach.

My first visit to the *OneTrackMinds* stage had me telling a story about an R. Kelly song.

Before you cancel me, this was 2017, and we didn't know the worst excesses of R. Kelly's behaviour then – but it was obviously a provocative choice for a feminist.

This is what it unlocked…

Happiness is an elusive quality, isn't it?

What is it? And why do we expect it? You often hear people say, 'I just want to be happy.' Or, 'I don't mind what my children do in life, as long as they're happy.' As if happiness is somehow easier to come by than success or money.

Happiness is what philosophers, poets and lovers have strived for throughout the history of humanity. Those same thinkers and writers accuse happiness of being fleeting. But happiness stays the same. We move the goalposts by wanting different things. You told happiness that if you could just be near him, next to her, in his life, in her bed, you'd never want anything else. You promised happiness just the sound of his voice, the smell of her neck, was all you'd ask for. Is it happiness's fault that the sound of the very same voice now irritates you beyond comprehension? Is happiness to blame that she gave you everything you wanted, and now you find your longed-for lover's inability to follow a logical argument infuriating when you once found it her most charming quality?

You thought love would bring you happiness. Instead it brought you fear, dread, loss and anguish. Love gifts you happiness in short, sharp, intense bursts, just enough to fool you into thinking it's the happiness courier, and makes you look in its post box for more.

Now perhaps you're wondering why R. Kelly's 'Remix to

Ignition' triggers a diatribe on happiness from me? There is a highly logical reason.

One night I was sitting on the sofa with my husband, Salinsky. (I often call him by his surname as if we are American TV cops.) He doesn't dance. I like to dance. This is only one of the various ways in which we are incompatible. He likes to make me laugh. He makes me feel funny. This is only one of the various ways in which we are highly compatible. Anyhow, the television was on. I flicked over to an MTV-style AllHitsAllDayAllOver music channel. We weren't really watching it. We were chatting. Joking. And he started to do a little head bob to the music, a neck dance, to make me laugh. He would never let another soul see him moving in this way. It was an intimate moment. A playful connection. I looked at him. Deadpan.

'Are you like R. Kelly, are you?'

'Yeah,' he said. Then after a beat, 'What's he like?'

It was then I realised that Salinsky did not know the singer on the television was R. Kelly. He was not cool enough to know that a man could have an R as a first name. That he'd said 'Yes' because he was a playful comedy improviser, trained to agree. And his curious brain had, a moment later, made him question what he'd agreed to – who he had claimed to be. This may well not be funny to you. But to me it was hysterical. I started to laugh. He started to laugh. And we could not stop. This was a moment of unbridled joy, affection, understanding, connection, engagement and togetherness to the exclusion of all others. This was a moment where our fears, doubts and worries were not welcome and knew there was no point even knocking. They left us alone. After twenty minutes of laughing at something no one else would really find terribly funny, as the giggles started to subside, I looked at Tom and said, 'This is it, you know... This is happy. This, right now on this sofa in these pyjamas. This joke will not be funnier in a bigger house, with more money in the bank, if we are more successful or celebrated. This. This is happy.'

'Let's get married,' he said.

And I heard happiness sigh. Because we'd tried to shut the window to keep her in. As if she couldn't walk through walls.

She comes to visit now and again. But rarely if we pine for her and never if we demand her. She almost always comes when the wifi is down, by way of replacement.

Because happiness – for all her faults – has got a delightful sense of humour.

Every time I visit *OneTrackMinds* as an audience member, I learn something about music and something about the individuals revealing themselves through their song choice. Every time I visit *OneTrackMinds* as a performer, I learn something about myself and reveal something I don't mean to. Music is a lifelong lover and companion. She can make you laugh, move and weep against your will. She will always make you remember. I hope this book inspires you to create a hundred playlists and walk down a city of memory lanes and see a myriad of new views from a familiar window.

Deborah Frances-White is a stand-up comedian, podcaster, screenwriter and corporate speaker. You may have heard her on *The Guilty Feminist* podcast, seen her on TV on *Have I Got News For You* or watched the film *Say My Name*, which she wrote.

Introduction

By Kristian Brodie

I know what you're thinking.

Can a song *really* change your life?

It's a question I get asked with uncommon frequency. And given that I've been curating and hosting a live storytelling show based entirely on this premise since 2016, you won't be surprised that my answer is always the same.

Yes. *Of course* a song can change your life. And I'll bet that a song has changed yours.

If I needed any proof to back up this claim, I can now point to the over 150 individuals who have taken up the challenge I set them when inviting them on to the show – to tell a story about a piece of music that has, in some way or other, changed their life. It could be a song that inspired their greatest work or soundtracked their lowest lows. It could be the song that was playing when they met the love of their life, or the song that reminds them of the one that got away.

Whatever their take on the brief – and over the years, those responses have been diverse and varied, as I hope this book will demonstrate – the results have been gloriously entertaining. A typical *OneTrackMinds* evening mixes the best parts of *Desert Island Discs*, TED Talks and *The Moth* – you'll hear some true stories, some great music, and perhaps you'll learn something as well. One of our guests, the poet and spoken-word artist Vanessa Kisuule, described our show as 'like stepping into a warm bath', which is a very gorgeous way of communicating all the things I love about doing *OneTrackMinds*. There's something very comforting about listening to people tell true stories – especially when they are as bold and brave as some of the ones we've heard – and the music works to enhance the emotional connection we have with each storyteller, allowing us to bond with them on a more sensual level as they share their track with us.

This book, then, is something of a snapshot of those past five years of doing the show at Wilton's Music Hall, Omeara London and various festivals around the country. We haven't been able to include all our favourites here – there simply wasn't enough room – but, together with my friend, co-presenter and co-editor Adam Shakinovsky, we went through a rigorous editing process to find twenty-five stories that we felt best represented what *OneTrackMinds* is all about. We've divided the stories in to four categories, which we feel broadly represent some of the main themes that have cropped up again and again since we started doing the show.

In Part 1, which we've called 'Becoming', there are stories of self-discovery, where a song has helped shape the path we take through life, and who we become as a result. Part 2 looks at stories of 'Belonging' – where a song has provided a sense of identity shared with a common group, and the subtle power that music has to make you feel part of a tribe. Part 3 – a little clumsily titled 'Beloving' – is made up of stories where that bond is even tighter – stories about songs that have made people fall in love, that have strengthened friendships and family bonds, and enhanced the power of relationships of all kinds. And finally, in Part 4, 'Believing', we have stories where music has acted as a salve, a solace, a reason to keep going.

All of these stories have been edited ever so slightly from their transcripts – mainly to remove off-the-cuff ad-libs or audience interactions – but always with a view to maintaining the spirit of the original oral nature of the story as much as possible.

You can read this book in order, or you can jump around between the chapters and curate your own *OneTrackMinds* night if you like. But, to echo my nannyish nagging from my role as host during the live shows, let me urge you to take the time to really listen to the songs as well. Treat them like we do in the live show – as an equal part of the presentation. We've tried to make this as easy for you as possible – the QR codes at the end of each story will take you to an online link where you'll be able to hear the song, and we've also put a full playlist on the onetrackminds.uk website.

But do, please, properly listen to the songs – while you're doing nothing else. Put your headphones on, close your eyes. Embrace the possibility of the life-changing power of music.

And perhaps one of these songs will change your life too.

Part 1 – Becoming

Jemima Foxtrot

This is a story about growing up through a muddled, muddy teenagerhood in Yorkshire; a Yorkshire replete with steep-sided valleys and bluebell woods, filled to the brim with newfound freedom and romance and drugs. This story is about how I found my lifelong love – funk and soul music.

I was fourteen when I met a couple of lads in my year at school, Louis and Jimmy. Two guitarists, music nerds. There was a music room at school, annexed off the back of the dining hall, and the three of us hung out together in there every single lunchtime. Knackered plastic keyboards lined the walls, and the carpet was flecked with chewing gum.

I had a tape of *Frank* by Amy Winehouse, which my dad had recorded for me off a CD from the library, and I also had a greatest hits of Ella Fitzgerald tape that I'd found in a charity shop the summer before. I'd listen to both of them religiously. When the boys weren't around – when they'd gone outside to smoke weed or whatever – I would stay in the music room and practise the scats until I had them down perfectly. Copying scats goes against the very essence of scats, but I didn't know that then and, even if I had, I wouldn't have cared.

It was just me, Jimmy and Louis at first, playing covers. Two guitars and a singer. We did Elton John's 'Your Song', which I couldn't fucking stand. Louis was responsible for the cheese. Louis and I were going out back then, and we were madly in love in that way that's specific to children. I stick by my childish loves; they were very, very real. Louis has remained a hefty romantic and he's got two kids of his own now. He's a singer/songwriter who writes and performs the most charming and buttery neo-soul you've ever heard.

I was drifting towards a howling kind of music because I was in awe of my own powerful voice. I liked singing stuff like Etta James and Little Richard, so I could enjoy my voice bouncing back at me from the walls of the music room, the bathroom and my own tender puberty.

Then came Calum. I knew Calum from Woodcraft Folk. I'm from Hebden Bridge and a lot of kids wind up attending Woodcraft Folk at some point. Calum was in the junior brass band that we used to laugh at every Christmas Eve when they played carols in the town square wearing their funny little suits. But also, and much more importantly, he played trombone and sax in this very cool ska band, where he was the youngest member.

Rehearsals moved to Louis' parents' front room. We had two guitars, one voice and a trombone, and we were so chuffed with ourselves. I was particularly happy with the brass. Brass creates sunshine. The sound of Calum's trombone and saxophone made me feel golden and warm. As if, when I swallowed it up, it lit something inside me that allowed me to glow.

Anyway, we needed a drummer. And good drummers are notoriously hard to find. We sloped around in our weird acoustic brass outfit for a while, playing open mics in village pubs and the like. Then one day in rehearsal, Calum said there was this girl in his year who had a little brother who played the drums. 'How little?' we asked him. Apparently the kid was two school years below us, which made him about twelve years old. We were naturally sceptical.

As I've said, we all lived in and around Hebden Bridge in the Pennines. It's beautiful there – open moors, dense woodland, a fairy tale of a place. I didn't appreciate it properly back then, all of that gasping, frantic landscape, but when I get to go back now, it's amazing. If you've never visited, you really should. Before it floods one too many times, before it's permanently underwater.

Our new potential drummer, Joe, lived halfway up the really steep hill that led up to my house. We all traipsed up there one Wednesday night. His parents opened the door; we shuffled in. They offered us tea and biscuits, all proud and polite, Joe looking at his trainers awkwardly. We went down to their basement, which housed the freezer, the washing machine, the cat-litter tray and, in the middle of it all, this basic three-piece turquoise drum kit.

We started playing 'Tutti Frutti' by Little Richard and Joe joined in. And he was fucking incredible. I was gobsmacked. It opened up so many windows in my soul, to attach my voice to this little kid who was giving us drums like thunder. I was blown away, and so were the rest of the band. He was in.

We started going up there regularly to practise and became really good friends. Joe was not your ordinary twelve-year-old. I credit Joe Ackroyd for introducing me – properly introducing me – to the musical genres that have played a really influential role in my work and in my development as an artist. The genres that I dance to, to this day, in my bedroom, in clubs, on the streets. The genres that I jog to on the Feld in Berlin, where I live now, under the giant and hopeful sky. The genres I've attached myself to like a limpet on a rock, the genres that validate me as a happy and optimistic person. Funk and soul.

An ex-boyfriend once said to me that he couldn't listen to a single funk or soul song with a female vocalist without thinking of me bouncing around, dancing, grinning from ear to ear. It's the music that's made me who I am, the music that's kept me alive.

For my eighteenth birthday – the band was still together, four years on – Joe made me a mix CD that he named *Flute Salad*. It was all no-nonsense, deep, ravenous female lead singers and all-consuming groove. The CD eventually got lost somewhere in one of my many changes of address. But I still carry loads of the tracks like glimmering jewels, warming me up, like talismans, like shields to protect me.

The band expanded – we gained a bassist called James – and we went on to claim five days' recording time in a local studio as the prize for winning the local 'Battle of the Bands'. We moved on from covers and wrote some pretty good pop songs. Eventually, James and Calum left, so it became me, Jimmy, Joe and Louis. And with a change of name, on we went.

The song that changed my life was one we played regularly early on in the band's career, when we were still doing covers. Joe suggested that we do this eager, howling song with its joyful, yearning energy. The version of this song that changed my life isn't the original by Cream. It's by Spanky Wilson. We were doing a cover of a cover. I remember struggling to reproduce the different version of the vocal on the chorus – the original was so ingrained. I almost gave up so many times in rehearsal, but Joe encouraged me, saying, 'No, come on! You can! You *have* to'.

The last time Joe, Jimmy, Louis and I were all together again was at our friend Jed's funeral in April 2015. He was twenty-five when he died. It was an unseasonably sunny day, and we all got sunburned drinking pints outside the pub by the canal.

Joe lives in Manchester now, currently building drum kits as his day job. He's a multi-instrumentalist in three bands whose genres range from psychedelic Latin to post-punk. He's about to start a degree in sound design. He's about to turn thirty. Grown up from a talented kid with the best taste in music to a man who breathes it brilliantly from every pore.

And I feel such a bond to him, and to the rest of the boys in the band. I don't have many friends left from secondary school, but they remain. And I know they always will. I'm eternally grateful to Joe for introducing me to a whole world of music through this one song. It's buoyed me up on so many occasions. And it's influenced not only my work as an artist, but my attitude towards the whole world.

When you listen to the track now, you'll notice that it starts with a very distinctive drumbeat. Whenever I hear that drumbeat, I think of Joe, child messiah, prophet of funk and soul, offering me my first hit of Spanky Wilson like a gateway drug. I think about teenaged me in that valley, breathing in all that music, and howling it right back out again.

'Sunshine of Your Love'
Written by Eric Clapton and Jack Bruce, with lyrics by Pete Brown
Performed by Spanky Wilson
Taken from the album *Doin' It*, released on Mothers Records
in 1969

YouTube

This was the first story ever told at the very first *OneTrackMinds* show at Wilton's Music Hall on 29 May 2016. As a beautiful piece of serendipity – which we didn't plan in any way – the next story that night was told by Pete Brown, a poet and lyricist, who wrote the lyrics to 'Sunshine of Your Love'.

Jemima Foxtrot is a writer, theatre-maker, performer and musician who creates and performs extensively, both nationally and internationally. Her first collection of poetry, *All Damn Day*, is published by Burning Eye Books. She's a founding member of the theatre company Unholy Mess.

Barry Adamson

The song that changed my life is a song of heartbreak. But, despite that, it's the song that put me on the career path that I've been on all my life.

I was thirteen years old. And in a way, you can say my puberty was born out of the absurd emotions that are in this song.

It was the school dance. I believed then – and maybe I still do, a little bit – that the way to secure a girl's heart was on the outside, by how you look. So in preparation, I went and bought myself a pair of Levi's Sta-Prest trousers, some oxblood loafers, a Ben Sherman checked shirt, and I finished it all off with a Crombie overcoat with a three-pointed handkerchief in the pocket and a fake-ass diamond right through the middle of it. This was going to do it for me.

I arrived at the dance and walked in. Already, the girls are all dancing around their handbags. And I'm dancing around them, trying to vie for attention. After all, I was wearing the sort of get-up that all the songs they were dancing to were all about.

The DJ played classic song after classic song – 'Hot Love' by T. Rex, 'Shaft', 'Me and You and a Dog Named Boo'. Ike and Tina Turner's 'Funkier Than a Mosquito's Tweeter'.

So things are warming up quite nicely.

And then suddenly, the lights go down. And the DJ says, 'Time to take your partners for the last dance... before I do.'

I mean, it was 1971, after all.

So, everybody looks around desperately. I see a girl in front of me. I make my way towards her. She gives me that look that I'd become accustomed to. An eye-roll, as if to say, 'Go on then... Why not, I suppose...'

Now, the song the DJ played – which is the song that changed my life – was 'Without You' by Harry Nilsson. It's a cover version of a British song by a group called Badfinger. They'd had a few minor hits before Harry Nilsson heard this song and thought, *I'd love to do that.*

So he went into the studio with his producer, Richard Perry. And they decided, with this song, with the components that are in there, that they could wring the emotional shit out of it and create a huge hit. Which is what they set out to do.

And so here I am at the school disco, coupled up. And this spooky piano starts, which, incidentally, the Carpenters borrowed many years later for their song 'Close to You'.

Now I hope you don't mind if I go off on one a little bit here about the mechanics of songwriting, because it is what I do, after all.

Harry Nilsson lays down a lyric on the top of that piano that sets out such emotional vulnerability from the get-go – there's a sort of patheticness (for want of a better word), but paradoxically at the same time there's a sense that, by admitting all these emotions, he's *really* in a position of power.

Back on the dance floor, we hold each other a little tighter.

The song continues. It's not ready for a chorus yet, so instead we get a second verse. This time, more instrumentation comes in and it all gets a little bit weird. Now the lyrics are talking about the future. And we're not sure if he likes this person he's singing to or not. The instrumentation gives us a few clues. The bass goes 'BRUUUFFHHH' all the way into the ground, followed by the strings chasing them.

By this time, I'm holding my dance partner like crazy. She's looking at me as if to say, 'What is going on!?'

I look left, I look right. Two girls have got their heads draped over much smaller boys' shoulders – and they're crying!

And I look at my not-so-significant other. And I say, 'What is this?'

And she looks back at me, her eyes full of understanding, and she says, 'It's the... song?'

And as the chorus kicks in, it's like a scene in a movie where the camera pans out and goes in at the same time, over the whole disco. And I'm sort of floating around, seeing the whole thing in this moment of wondrous clarity. Because at that moment, I know – *this* is what I'm going to do! *This* is the way to communicate to people! It's not with this Crombie overcoat at all.

And Harry sings the chorus, and then he starts to *screech* it out. At the top of his voice. He spits it out, over everyone, in an act of desperation.

And that's it, really. The song should end there. It's only one minute, forty-one seconds up to that point. But it would work.

The story goes that the two guys in Badfinger, who originally wrote the song, came at it from completely different places. One of them had written a chorus, and the other one had a verse. So they call each other up.

And one says, 'I've got a verse.'

And the other replies, 'Really? I've got a chorus!'

So they put those two together. And that was it.

At this point in a song, as a writer, what you'd typically do is try and relieve the listener a little bit. Maybe you'd write a middle eight, take the song somewhere else before coming back.

But no.

Oh no.

This is a very troubled song. We're only halfway through. And they know that they shouldn't do this, but...

They play the whole thing through again.

And at an *elevated* level.

More harmonies!

More strings!

More brass!

They *will* feel my pain!

And as listeners we're tied to the track because we want resolution! It's a story, after all. We want an ending, we want closure. So we're hanging in there while it's all going on. First verse repetition, and then an extended chorus over and over and over.

And what does Harry do?

He leaves us.

His voice gets faded out in the mix. It goes off into oblivion, leaving us with his sense of abandonment.

What happens next is this genius piece of production from Richard Perry. The strings and brass get together – the brass provide these slabs of stabbing articulation, and the strings run for mercy out of the room. And this conflict creates two contrary emotions, bringing about a resolve that moves the piece towards an ending, towards that resolution as it moves away and fades into nothingness.

Back on the dance floor, we feel complete.

I look at my partner, and it's clear that she sees that something has happened to me. That I have undergone a change.

The lights came up. Everybody shuffled around. The boys tried to fight each other. The girls got together to discuss which boys were hot and which ones were not.

And the DJ said, 'On your way out, please make sure you've got all your belongings... before I do.'

It was 1971, after all...

'Without You'
Written by Pete Ham and Tom Evans
Performed by Harry Nilsson
Taken from the album *Nilsson Schmilsson*, released by RCA in 1971

Apple Music   Spotify

This story was first performed at Wilton's Music Hall on 14 February 2018.

Barry Adamson is a musician, composer, writer, photographer and film-maker. He was part of the seminal 1970s post-punk band Magazine and later a founding member of Nick Cave's legendary band the Bad Seeds. He's worked with David Lynch, Depeche Mode, Danny Boyle and the Jon Spencer Blues Explosion, and was nominated for a Mercury Music Prize for his album *Soul Murder*.

Patrick Gale

So, it was 1979. I was seventeen. And I was a virgin.

I'd finished my A levels, and I had a long summer ahead of me, working in Moles Café for £25 a week and preparing for my Oxbridge exam by reading the complete works of George Eliot. None of my friends were around because I was one of the few day boys in a boarding school. I had friends. I even had gay friends – which was pretty amazing, given that homosexuality between consenting adults had only been legal for about a decade. We were out and proud, and a merry gang of five, but none of them lived in Winchester. So it was just me and George.

None of them was a virgin either, because all-male boarding schools are basically like prisons, in that nobody willing, with a pulse, has to go very long without sex. In fact, if you're unwilling, and don't have a pulse... well, never mind...

At this moment in time, the sporty one was off sulking in Oxfordshire; the quiet one and the outrageous judgemental one were off in Greece discovering ancient civilisations, because they were classicists; and my bestie, who was in London, was preparing to drop us all, go straight, get married and become a High Court judge. You may hiss.

But then I ran into our headmaster, who was a lover of the arts, and he must have read the situation pretty well, because he conjured up a miraculous travel scholarship for me. So I went off with a Eurail Pass on a train to Athens.

In those days, this journey took quite a while, as it involved four different trains and a boat. I had an evening in Paris, a whole day in Venice, a whole night being shaken awake by communist Hildegards in Yugoslavia, and by the time we got to Athens I was still a virgin.

Quiet Complacent and Outrageous Judgemental were very pleased to see me because, along with *Daniel Deronda*, I'd bought a larger tent than theirs, a camping stove, two saucepans, a kettle and Elizabeth David's *Mediterranean Cookery*. For three weeks we were really very good (even though they smoked unfiltered Gauloises) and we saw every museum and archaeological site in Athens, Nafplion, Mycenae, Delphi and Olympia. But in the last week – because it's the only way you can see the magnificent remains at Delos, unless you have a yacht – we went to Mykonos.

That's right – a place so gay that men in moustaches hand out lube and Armistead Maupin novels as you disembark.

We stayed in a clothing-optional campsite, full of gentlemen who were very pleased to see three seventeen-year-olds with limited spending money. Needless to say, in every photograph of that week I am fully dressed and defending my honour with *Felix Holt*. (That's not a body spray: it's a very long political novel by George Eliot).

Quiet Complacent copped off with a peripatetic music teacher from Dorking. Outrageous Judgemental claimed he'd copped off with a crazily hot but strangely invisible gap-year student with his own boat.

I remained a virgin.

On the last night, though, we had to sleep on the beach in town, because the ferry for Athens left before the first boat from our campsite. And something in me just flipped. I left the others to guard my bags and announced that I was off to see a man about a cherry.

To be fair, they were so flabbergasted, it didn't occur to them to come along and cramp my style. I headed straight to the main gay bar, propped myself up on the wall outside with a bottle of Fanta and waited.

I had absolutely no idea how to cruise. But my big sister had said that in a photograph where I was really scowling, I looked like the hero on a Barbara Cartland cover. So I frowned when anyone I fancied came near.

Eventually, an extremely handsome man who looked about thirty bought me a G & T. And because he was from Paris, where everyone is famously rude, he must have thought the scowl was a bit of a come-on. And just at the moment when we started to kiss, and my head filled with the scent of his Eau Savage and after-sun, this bloody song came on...

It's an incredibly cheesy song, lent an added irony, I've since discovered, by having been originally conceived to be suggestively performed by an eleven-year-old with a telephone. But it was apt.

He lived nearby, and the song followed us up the alley and up the steps to his little holiday flat. My heart was thumping and I felt incredibly grown-up.

He was called Christian, and he couldn't have been more perfect, even though he kept on singing 'Winchester Cathedral' once he'd worked out what my home town was. And we had to use Ambre Solaire because, strangely, he didn't have any lube, and it stings... And despite the fact that the coffee he brought me in bed the following morning was only instant. He was tender and passionate, even though I just lay there like a primeval fish.

He gave me his address in Paris, said we should meet again, made a nice show, as we kissed one last time on his doorstep, of nearly making me miss my ferry, and as far as I was concerned, my bell had been rung. I was in love.

Needless to say, I was insufferable all the way back to Athens, and the others were furious with me. But I was invincible. I was in love, I was no longer a virgin, and I had finished *Felix Holt*.

That night, on the roof of our youth hostel in Athens, as the inevitable American girls sang softly to their guitars, I sat up to write Christian four very witty sides of onion-skin about myself, my hopes, my dreams...

To my delight and the huge irritation of my friends, I had a brief letter back from him at the start of the new term. His tone was a little more cautious than mine, but then he was a sophisticated adult, and I was only a schoolboy. I wrote back at greater length. I enthused about George Eliot and Oxford, but also about how I might flunk Oxbridge and come to Paris instead and study to be an actor. I was a good cook, I said, and very tidy. He didn't reply.

Outrageous Judgemental acquired the single of our song and played it whenever I came to his study for coffee. He told me to write again, but in salacious French, which he dictated. This time my last two letters were returned. They'd been opened and resealed, and an official stamp said that Christian was unknown at that address.

A year later, when we were both university students, Outrageous Judgemental and I went to Paris, and at his insistence we tracked down the address, somewhere in the Seizième.

It turned out not to be a private house at all, but a place where they trained Catholic priests who then took vows of celibacy. Possibly this explains the odd lack of lube. Outrageous Judgemental, who has not mellowed with time but remains a very dear friend to this day, said it was not the first and certainly not the last time I would find myself fucked by God...

22

'Ring My Bell'
Written by Frederick Knight
Performed by Anita Ward
Taken from the album *Songs of Love*, released on T. K. Records
in 1979

Apple Music

Spotify

This story was first performed at Wilton's Music Hall on 25 April 2019.

Patrick Gale is one of the UK's most beloved novelists. His works include *Rough Music, Ease, Notes from an Exhibition* and *Take Nothing With You*. He is the chairman of the North Cornwall Book Festival and a patron of the Penzance LitFest. He lives in Cornwall with his husband and a herd of beef cattle, and his chief extravagance in life is opera tickets.

Kristian Brodie

I am in Los Angeles. Santa Monica, to be more exact. To be even more precise, I am in a weirdly outdated 1970s fever dream of a hotel room, in the Loews Hotel. The suite – all beige carpets and faux-wood panelling – has been converted for our purposes into an office, and I am wearing a poorly fitting blue suit and an ill-matching off-the-rack shirt that I bought just days earlier. I am jet-lagged to an unreasonable degree, and I am doing my best to appear in control.

I am at the American Film Market – the place where one's ideas that the film industry is in any way glamorous go to die. And I am a film sales agent – a job I am perhaps ill cut out for at this point in my young life, not least because it's a job I didn't know existed two months earlier. This is my first business trip, and aside from being unrested and nervous, I am trying desperately not to look like I don't know what I am doing. Which is a problem. Because I don't know what I am doing.

Not really. I have been given only the briefest briefings of what is expected of me, and I would be lying now, as I was lying then, if I said that I fully understood precisely what I'd been asked to do. Moreover, I'm not entirely sure *why* I am doing what I'm doing. On

24

this, our first morning of the first day of my first sales market, the futility of the next week seems to rise up and slap me in the face.

Every day for the next five days I will spend the hours of 8 a.m. to 6 p.m. in this bizarre time warp of a hotel room. The company I work for has a slate of films, ranging from low-budget horror flicks to grossly indulgent art-house dramas, with the only thing uniting them being that almost certainly nobody will ever watch them. Every half-hour a new buyer will come in, and I will have less than thirty minutes to tell them about the films we have available in their territory and which ones they should definitely buy from us. Because I am new to this, I have been charged with selling to the territories that bear little responsibility for our company's overall success. But I need to learn the ropes, and so I am given what are euphemistically referred to as 'the minor territories'. All the big hitters in the international box office are mine – Bulgaria, Malaysia, Peru, Iceland. It's fairly clear from my first few meetings that none of my clients have any money and no one is terribly interested in what I am telling them. The challenge ahead of me feels insurmountable.

I took this job because it seemed like some sort of opening into the film industry – however tangential, however far removed from the actual process of making films. For many years I had had some poorly thought through ambitions to work in film, to be a film-maker of sorts – a writer, perhaps, or maybe a producer. But I'd never had anything like the courage to put my dreams into action, or done anything to suggest that I had the skill set – or the talent – to get me there.

In film, the first such step is usually getting a job in the mail room of a talent agency, but I'd already tried that and been fired after three months. So trying my hand as a sales agent seemed like a good next step. A step in the right direction.

And it was. After all, selling – especially selling films – is a creative act. To a great degree, it's storytelling. And like any good storyteller, I had to be engaging, to get the key points across succinctly and entertainingly. I had to know my audience. I had to give them what they wanted.

That year our slate was dominated by a massive new project, the biggest film our small company had ever taken on to sell. It was an epic, multi-generational romantic drama, with a monumental £20 million budget, that had all the hallmarks of a modern independent cinematic classic.

The film was directed by the late, great Richard Attenborough, a veritable legend of cinema. The cast was A-list all the way – Oscar winners Shirley MacLaine, Christopher Plummer and Pete Postlethwaite; Neve Campbell and Mischa Barton (straight out of *The O.C.*). The story was a cracker too – a heartbreaking but ultimately uplifting romance set against the backdrop of the Second World War.

It was, for this young first-time salesman, a veritable gimme. Within hours I felt my confidence grow as I leaned into the pitch and started getting interest from buyers.

To make my job even easier, we had been sent a knockout twelve-minute promotional trailer, and it was jam-packed with big-money shots, all designed perfectly to get buyers pulling out their chequebooks. There was romance, there was excitement, there was entirely unnecessary nudity (this was, alas, long before Me Too, and I'm sorry to say that an entirely fatuous scene where Mischa Barton appears completely naked for no credible reason whatsoever was deemed a highly sellable asset). It culminated in a final ninety seconds packed full of explosions and plane crashes, and 'Oscar winner Shirley MacLaine' in big letters across the screen, and more nudity and kisses... all soundtracked by the song 'Because of You' by Kelly Clarkson.

Now, up until that point in my life, it's fair to say that I had been fairly sniffy about Miss Clarkson and her oeuvre, dismissing it as a load of Simon Cowell-flavoured *X-Factor/American Idol* bollocks. But as a wise man once said, context is everything, and in this case the context – the previously described gloriously over-the-top trailer – made *all* the difference. Never before had the marriage of music and imagery been more perfectly matched! That song – all big lungs and high notes and teary lyrics and bombastic chord changes – was the aural equivalent of the promo it was soundtracking.

I was under strict instructions to play the trailer to every single buyer who came in for a meeting. So that clip – and that song – played at least once every thirty minutes from 8 a.m. to 6 p.m. every day for five days. It was inescapable. It had taken up residency in my brain.

And in the end it became my victory anthem. Because I sold the shit out of that film! I got behind the pitch with all my youthful energy and passion. 'This film,' I told my buyers, 'is going to be huge. It's going to win all the awards. It's going to appeal to all four quadrants, male and female, old and young.'

'This film,' I said, 'is going to be a love story for the ages.'

'This film,' I said, 'is going to be the next *Titanic*.'

And the offers came in, and we pushed them higher, and the deals were done, and I ended the market with a remarkable first market haul of sales for our company, and we went out for dinner to a fancy restaurant on our last night in LA, and my boss raised a glass to me, and I felt like I had arrived...

Now's probably a good time to tell you that I hadn't seen the film yet.

We were pre-selling it, trying to get some sales in the can so that the producers could complete the post-production and secure festival slots for its release. So all of the passion for the film that I'd imbued my pitches with had come from the enthusiasm of my boss, this incredibly persuasive trailer and, you know, Kelly Clarkson.

Two weeks later I'm back in London, and an invitation arrives in my inbox to a screening of the film that evening. I am ridiculously excited. I cannot wait to see this masterpiece that I'd been so eloquently passionate about a fortnight earlier.

The screening room was packed. The producers were there. Some of the cast were there. Richard Attenborough was there. This was the moment it started to feel real. I'd taken this job full of hope, but I'd never expected that, three months later, I'd be in a screening room with proper Hollywood actors and a genuine cinematic legend of a director, about to watch a film that I could legitimately say I'd had some part (albeit a very small one) in creating. I pinched myself.

I was a part of this.

And here was my reward.

I took a seat. The lights went down, the curtain went back, the film started... and almost immediately it was obvious that it was terrible. Utterly, utterly terrible. Within minutes it became very clear to me – and probably, if they were being honest to themselves, everyone else in the room – that this was a great steaming turd of a movie.

Everything about it was awful.

The performances were abject.

The dialogue was clichéd nonsense.

The romance was entirely unbelievable.

The plot was preposterous.

The explosions and the plane crashes, which had looked so great in the promo, looked so shoddy here.

The utterly unnecessary nudity seemed all the more seedy...

Eventually, mercifully, it ended, and as the credits started to roll, I got out of my chair and slipped out of the room before the lights went up, desperate to avoid having to see anyone, having to awkwardly pretend that this piece of garbage was remotely worthy of praise.

And as I ran up the stairs to the street, all my lines from that Loews Hotel room – all my *lies* – came back to me.

This was a masterpiece.

This was going to win all the Oscars.

This was a guaranteed box-office smash.

This was the next Titanic.

(I suppose I was right about that last one, in that it ended up being a complete fucking disaster – but that wasn't what I meant at the time.)

Out on the street the skies had opened, and a cold torrent of November rain greeted me. And without even stopping to think, I walked out into the rain and let it wash over me.

Because at that moment I felt like I needed some penance. I needed some punishment. I was going to walk home, and I was going to let the rain cleanse away my shame.

I don't think I knew it immediately, but with hindsight I can pinpoint that cold wet walk through Fitzrovia as the moment where a seed was sown for me. The passion and energy I'd felt for this film excited me so much, but the deflation I'd felt in that screening room made me realise that I couldn't sell what I didn't believe in. I knew that it would never be enough for me to tell other people's stories if I didn't believe in them.

I stuck around in that job for another two and a half years, but my heart was never in sales ever again. My brief love affair with that line of work fizzled out in less time than the promo for that terrible movie.

And that stupid, stupid song, whose words now echoed in my head.

After about ten minutes of walking (all the time making sure not to stray too far from the sidewalk) I was soaked to the skin, absolutely freezing, and my youthful sense of self-pity and eagerness for wallowing had been replaced by a fairly urgent need to get out of the rain. I'd done enough penance for my liking, and so I hailed a cab.

As I jumped in the back of the taxi and wriggled my way out of my now sodden coat, I noticed that the radio was on.

And I wonder now if you'll believe me if I told you that the song that was playing at that very minute, as the cab pulled away into the night, was that same, abhorrent, mocking bastard of a song that had got me into this state in the first place...

'Because of You'
Written by Kelly Clarkson, David Hodges and Ben Moody
Performed by Kelly Clarkson
Taken from the album *Breakaway*, released on RCA Records
in 2005

Apple Music   Spotify

This story was first performed at Omeara London on 27 February 2019.

Kristian Brodie is the founder, producer and host of *OneTrackMinds*.
He works in London as a story and development executive for film
and TV. He has produced two feature films – the BIFA-award
winning documentary *Next Goal Wins* and the BAFTA-winning
Beast. He lives in Walthamstow with his wife, their daughter and
their Shiba Inu named Kenji.

Steve Chapman

In 1965 George Harrison's dentist famously introduced the Beatles to LSD – a mind-altering substance that irrevocably changed their music and turned a generation of Beatles fans on to experimental psychedelia. Twelve years later, Neil Innes and Eric Idle released a spoof biopic about the Beatles called *The Rutles*. However, in this story it isn't a dentist but Bob Dylan who introduces the band to a mind-altering substance. And the mind-altering substance isn't LSD but tea. Subsequent tea-drinking sessions and late-night tea parties irrevocably changed the music of the Rutles and turned a generation of Rutles fans on to experimental hot leaf infusions.

Now, the song that changed my life isn't by the Beatles or the Rutles, but it is a story that involves me and a certain mind-altering substance that I'm rather ashamed to talk about. So, to preserve my dignity over the next few pages, whenever you hear me mention the word 'tea', or if I tell you that somebody offered me a cup of 'tea', or that I drank so much 'tea' I melted my brain – you know what I'm *really* talking about...

Fast forward to the summer of 1983. Eleven-year-old me was in that wonderful sweet spot between primary and secondary school. Even at this tender young age I had a good sense of who I was and what I wanted to be in the world. I was Steve the DJ – host of my own bedroom radio show that I recorded on my little Sanyo tape recorder. With a limited vinyl collection, much of which I borrowed from my parents, I specialised in playing a weirdly random mix of music. I didn't care if I played the Rolling Stones followed by Chas 'n' Dave followed by the England World Cup Squad with 'This Time (We'll Get it Right)'. Every now and then I'd intersperse this strange cacophony of tunes with competitions where you could ring in and win prizes such as stroking my dog or marrying my younger brother. I didn't care that nobody was actually listening.

Not only was I a DJ, I was also Steve the multi-instrument-playing musician. I knew three chords on my little half-sized guitar and would regularly compose bizarre instrumental numbers on my old battery-operated keyboard, which sounded like a hovercraft when it was switched on. I was chuffed that I had already played my first gig, having been invited to perform a strange self-composed Kraftwerk-esque number in school assembly, while the other kids played an ensemble of 'Frère Jacques' on the recorder.

But the thing I was most proud of was that I was Steve the artist and illustrator, creator of a collection of short stories about a character called Yappy Dog – stories that my wonderfully supportive teachers would let me write in class and later encourage me to read to the younger kids. And, having written a number of well-received comedy sketches for the final end-of-term play, I left primary school on a creative high, excited about developing my talents further when I started big school that September.

So it came as a bit of a shock when I arrived at secondary school only to discover that nobody was interested in any of these things, especially the teachers. In fact, the first lesson that secondary school taught me was that the creative superpowers I had spent the last six years nurturing were of no use in the adult world. At best, they were cute hobbies that had to be confined to the weekends when I didn't have homework to do. At worst, they were dangerous distractions from the more important work that I was now to focus my attention on: subjects such as maths, English and history, which were taught in a way that simply didn't work for an easily distracted dyslexic lad like me, who thought in patterns and tangents. And then came the ritual humiliation of exams – anxiety-inducing memory tests that I simply wasn't wired to be any good at. So, having started secondary school with a good sense of who I was and what I wanted to be, I left not knowing the answer to either of those questions, my mediocre exam grades hanging around my neck as a constant reminder that I was neither intelligent nor creative. Aged eighteen and not knowing what to do with myself, I left school and got a job in a factory packing boxes.

It was around this time that music became very important to me. Having lost a sense of who I was, I started to look to music to try and find some form of identity. I wanted to find a band or a genre where I felt like I fitted in. In fact, I think this all began in the latter stages of secondary school, where for some reason I decided I wanted to be Francis Rossi of Status Quo. This was probably because the Quo had featured regularly on my bedroom radio playlist back in the glory days and, as I knew three chords on my guitar, I could play much of their back catalogue. I grew my hair long and started to wear a dangerous amount of denim. But it had the opposite effect. Instead of finding myself, I simply felt more of an imposter. Worse still, my friends became somewhat embarrassed by my gangly, denim-clad appearance, and it certainly wasn't having the desired effect on the teenage girls who were starting to catch my eye.

I realised that this wasn't working but in hindsight took a bit of a wrong turn when I decided I was going to up my game by becoming a heavy-metal rock god. Out went the Quo and in came bands like

Guns 'n' Roses, AC/DC and Metallica. The hair grew longer and various patches were sewn onto my denim jacket. I even bought a pair of studded leather gloves that I would wear on the walk to and from school – a look that in retrospect was probably more S & M than rock and roll.

It was during this rather confused heavy-metal phase that I was spat out of the secondary schooling system and into the factory – a rather tough, male-dominated environment in which a shy, long-haired young lad made an easy target for good-natured piss-taking. But the factory wasn't all bad. Shift work meant that I started to earn a decent amount of money, and as many of my mates had gone off to university, I would spend my hard-earned cash going to visit different campuses each weekend. One weekend I'd be at John Moore's in Liverpool, the next in Southampton, then on to Brighton, London or Northampton. The greatest thing about these trips was that they introduced me to a plethora of new music that I hadn't yet encountered: shoegaze bands such as My Bloody Valentine, the Jesus and Mary Chain and Spacemen 3, the tail end of the Madchester scene with the Happy Mondays and Stone Roses, and the embryonic beginnings of Britpop with Blur, Oasis and Pulp. I cut my hair and traded the denim for baggy jumpers, black jeans and T-shirts emblazoned with obscure bands such as Pop Will Eat Itself and Carter the Unstoppable Sex Machine.

And it was on one of these university trips that somebody offered me a cup of 'tea'. I'd heard of 'tea' and knew of its long association with music, so I thought I'd try it while watching Spiritualized live at UEA in Norwich. And, just like it did for the Beatles (and the Rutles), 'tea' changed my relationship to music for ever. But while seeing Spiritualized live was an amazing experience, it was actually the music played by the DJ beforehand that captivated me – a mix of psychedelic/alternative bands such as the 13th Floor Elevators, MC5, the Velvet Underground and, for the first time, I heard all nine minutes and forty-one seconds of Pink Floyd's 'Interstellar Overdrive'. And it was here that I found my next musical crush. Mr Syd Barrett.

I knew right away I couldn't compete with Syd in the sartorial department. I'd made that mistake with denim and I certainly wasn't going to repeat it with crushed velvet and paisley. And there was no way I could imitate Syd's wonderfully voluminous curly locks with my rather lank, perfectly straight hair. I decided the best way I could become more like Syd was to emulate his legendary love of 'tea'.

Had I known at the time the full extent of Syd's life story, I would have realised this was a very bad idea. But it seemed to work for a while. Whenever the opportunity arose, I'd have a cup of 'tea' and it would make me feel more like Syd. I started a weird psychedelic band called Reverberation, and with each cup of Earl Grey or Oolong I began to develop a rather whimsical and wonky perspective on the world. But one day I had must have had a dodgy batch of Darjeeling, and it all went wrong. I sipped one cup of 'tea' too many and broke my brain, entering a very dark three-month period of depression, paranoia, shame and guilt. In my pursuit to find out who I was, I had ended up so far away from myself that I was now hopelessly lost.

The factory wasn't a great place to be experiencing this embarrassing mental disintegration, but it was there that I found an ally in the form of a young Irish lad called Brendan. Brendan was a student at university in Dublin who was working in the factory during the summer holidays, and I soon learned that we had a similar love of music. (I also suspected Brendan was a 'tea' drinker, so would be sympathetic towards my mild psychosis.) But while Brendan was also a fan of Syd, his music tastes were much broader than mine, and I was delighted when he handed me a homemade mix tape, which he had named *Various Savouries*. The little C90 cassette lived up to its name and introduced me to a diverse range of new bands such as Half Japanese, Can, Mercury Rev and many more. But there was one song on the tape that stopped me in my tracks and made me shout, 'WTF!' or whatever we said to that effect in 1993.

The song began with what sounded like a bad recording of a talking kid's toy. This was followed by a creepy keyboard that was reminiscent of my weird old hovercraft organ. Then, out of the silence, an odd childlike voice appeared and said, 'Hi, how are you?'

What followed was three and a half minutes of music that I couldn't tell if I loved or hated, but that I couldn't stop listening to. Brendan had returned to Ireland and I'd lost the handwritten inlay card, so I had no idea what this song was, other than it came on after 'Our Singer' by Pavement. I had to find out who this mysterious musician was. I played the song to music-loving friends in the hope they would be able to shed some light on the mystery, but they just laughed and suggested that the song had been recorded by Brendan himself as a joke.

As email hadn't yet become a thing, I decided to write a letter to Brendan, and a few weeks later I got a reply. Brendan explained that the mystery song was called 'Walking the Cow' by an Austin-based singer-songwriter called Daniel Johnston. He went on to tell me that Daniel was largely unknown but had a loyal cult following due to his simplistic and very lo-fi style. In fact, when Daniel created his early albums, he had no means of reproducing them, so used to play them over and over again for each individual tape. Brendan also told me about Daniel's shadow side. His demons. That he was a paranoid schizophrenic plagued by an obsession with the devil. That he had been arrested a number of times and was continuously in and out of various psychiatric institutions.

And, on hearing all of this, I fell in love with Daniel. But, unlike with Syd and Axl and Francis (and all the others), I didn't want to *become* him. Instead I fell in love with what he stood for. I fell in love with his innocence. With his simplicity. With the way in which he expressed his pain and passion through creating raw music and tender art. From the moment I learned about the man behind the music, Daniel become a hero of mine. The perfect outsider.

I listen to Daniel's music often. It reminds me that there is beauty in simplicity. That feeling like an outsider isn't something to be ashamed of but something uniquely wonderful to embrace and nurture. He taught me that heroes come in many forms and that it is often the most ordinary and unremarkable who have the power to most inspire. But the biggest gift Daniel gave me was the invitation to make again, just for the sake of making. To make *art* simply for the sake of making art. To make *music* simply for the sake of making music. To embrace passionate, uncensored creative expression as simply part of what it means to be human. Daniel's music constantly reunites me with that eleven-year-old kid who used to write those Yappy Dog books, broadcast radio shows to nobody and play weird hovercraft organ music in school assembly.

Daniel died suddenly in September 2019, just three weeks before I was due to meet him at his home in Texas. I learned of his passing while on a train journey, and an unexpected wave of grief suddenly washed over me, making me realise just how important he had become to me over the years and how pivotal that weird song on that old mix tape had been. So, I dedicate this story to Daniel. Thank you. And wherever you are, 'Hi, how are you?'

'Walking the Cow'
Written by Daniel Johnston
Performed by Daniel Johnston
Taken from the album *Hi, How Are You*, released on Stress Records
in 1983

Apple Music   Spotify

This story was first performed at the House of St Barnabas on 16 May 2019.

Steve Chapman (www.canscorpionssmoke.com @stevexoh) is an artist, writer and speaker interested in creativity and the human condition. He has spoken around the world about human creativity, has exhibited his artwork alongside the likes of Pablo Picasso and David Shrigley and sold his work across five continents. He is at his best when he is not quite sure what he is doing.

Joan Iyiola

When I was first asked about which song changed my life, I knew immediately which group I wanted to write about. And just as immediately, I swallowed the idea again, trying instead to force out something more worthy of the brief, a seminal theme tune of my life. There was a part of my music-loving adult self that thought that my instant and instinctual choice wasn't highbrow enough for *OneTrackMinds*.

I mean, my chosen song is a little bit trashy. But I really love it. When I last checked, this track had 312,854,844 plays on Spotify. Which is way more than the most-played Beatles song or the most-played Rolling Stones song. And that made me feel a little bit better about my choice.

I've started to encounter something incredibly interesting in my work as an actress. Over the last few weeks, a couple of white male directors in their forties offered me some feedback as to why I didn't get a particular job this time around. And while they said some *lovely* things, their reasoning was that they had decided to go for someone who is... more *fragile* as a person.

Which is wild, right?

To make sense of this, we have to take the story further back – to the 1990s – 1996, to be precise.

A lot happened in 1996. I was nine years old. Fergie and Andrew got a royal divorce. Take That split up (for a little while, anyway). Dolly the cloned sheep was 'born'. Three lions were on our shirts as Terry Venables took England to the semi-finals of Euro 96. Everyone thought that we were going to run out of oil. It was the last year of Tory rule for thirteen years. Imagine.

My primary school wasn't insanely conservative, but it was unbelievably tame. My friends and I were always being told to use our 'inside voices', even when we were outside. To cross our legs so we didn't show our knickers. To not agitate the boys.

And then, in July of 1996, we were introduced to Ginger, Baby, Sporty, Scary and Posh. They were half big sisters, half superheroes. And something in my understanding of the world changed the moment I encountered them for the first time.

The characters in the storybooks that I read didn't look like the friends that I had made. In my dreams as a child, everyone was white.

Which is wild, right?

That began to change when the Spice Girls arrived.

Given the fact that one of them looked a bit like me – and had a thing for wearing leopard print – I knew my time had come. They were so *different*.

My friends and I quickly assembled our tribute band. Joanna was Baby. She was the youngest of the group. Geri was Geri (it was a natural fit). Lisa and Frankie always fought over who was going to be Posh, and whoever lost that week had to be Sporty. And I was Scary. In a sea of misfits, the school halls finally felt like home.

I had all the merch. I collected the Pepsi ring-pulls and covered everyone with Spice Girls Impulse body spray. And armed with all of that tat and our thrown-together costumes, we performed for every classroom and at every summer fete that would allow us to.

That Mel B embraced her natural hair meant young women of colour could look up to their favourite pop group and see an idol. Were the Spice Girls flawed? My God, yes. But that Mel B understood the wash-and-leave-in routine was unbelievable to me.

And then there was her famous tongue piercing. But with my Nigerian parents, that was never going to happen.

I did take all of this new-found empowerment a little too far one time, when I said, 'Are you alrigh', mate?' to my dad.

To which he curtly replied, 'I am not your mate. I am your father.'

There was one day that my brother made me lose my temper by trying to turn off the Spice Girls album just as I was practising their latest dance routine. He wanted hip-hop; I wanted Spice Girls. The fighting led us to the kitchen, and as he pushed me into the oven door, I found a frying pan, cracked it on his head and resumed swinging and shaking to 'Who Do You Think You Are?'

And then there was the playground incident... While my friends and I were mid-rehearsal, we noticed that some boys in the year above had just discovered the new girl, and they were starting to pick on her. Just as the Avengers assemble in a Marvel movie, we descended in our group and circled the bullies. And we just started singing at them. Not even singing, really, we were *shouting* at them. Shouting the lyrics of every Spice Girl song that we knew off by heart. It must have been frightening for us at the time. But it worked. They never bothered anyone again. And the new girl, Prita, came on to Team Spice. So then we were six. Which was a bit awkward...

But girl power for us was never about putting other people down to feel better. It taught us all how to support each other, despite our differences. I mean, Nelson Mandela called the Spice

Girls his heroes! Even after Mel B told him that she sneaked some loo roll from his house into her pocket.

Which is wild, right?

The Spice Girls shaped a generation. And they instilled so much confidence in me. So to the next casting director who is looking for someone more fragile, here's my response. Spice up your life.

'Wannabe'
Written by the Spice Girls, Matt Rowe and Richard Stannard
Performed by the Spice Girls
Taken from the album *Spice*, released on Virgin Records in 1996

Apple Music   Spotify

This story was first performed at Wilton's Music Hall on 7 February 2019.

Joan Iyiola is an artist, an actress, a writer and a producer. Her credits as an actress include *Black Earth Rising* (BBC/Netflix), *New Blood* (BBC/Netflix), *Tree* (Young Vic) and *The Duchess of Malfi* (Royal Shakespeare Company). She is a co-founder of the Mono-Box, a non-profit organisation supporting emerging artists in theatre and film.

Peter Tatchell

There are many music tracks that have influenced me and inspired me. There are many I could have chosen to write about here. But the track I've chosen for this story – the track that perhaps helped shape my life – is 'To Be Young, Gifted and Black' by the fabulous Nina Simone.

Now, if you know me, you may be asking yourself, *What's that got to do with him? He's not Black.*

It's a long story. And like all long stories, it starts with once upon a time...

In 1963, when I was eleven, I remember hearing about the bombing of a Black church in Birmingham, Alabama, where four young girls, about my own age, were murdered. I can remember thinking, even as an eleven-year-old, *How could anyone kill another human being, let alone four young girls? In church. On Sunday morning.*

I was horrified. I cried. They were just kids like me. And that inspired my interest in and support for the Black civil rights movement. The US was a faraway country. I was living in Melbourne, Australia at the time. But I made this connection, that the rights of all of us are interconnected, and that we have a duty to support all people everywhere who are suffering injustice.

I grew up in a very evangelical Pentecostal family. My father was a factory worker, and my mother was mostly a housewife, though she sometimes worked in the local biscuit factory. All our life revolved around the family and the church. We only had three books in the house. One was an atlas. One was the Bible. And one was a book of Bible prophecies. I didn't have much in the way of horizons or expectations, but for some reason I connected with what was happening to Black people in America. I saw this as a terrible wrong. And I could particularly relate to the civil rights struggle because one of the leaders of that movement, Martin Luther King, was a Baptist minister. And in my own childlike way, being brought up in this deeply Christian family, I could relate to his activism as the expression of the true principles of Christ's gospel. Love thy neighbour as thyself. Be a Good Samaritan. Blessed are the peacemakers. I am my brother's (and sister's) keeper.

So I used to follow every single newspaper, TV and radio account about the Black civil rights movement. I was truly inspired. I thought to myself, *This is what Christianity should be.* Not just pious words and prayers, but social activism, to get as close to heaven as we can on earth. To make those principles espoused in the Sermon on the Mount our reality here and now.

It wasn't until some years later, when I was seventeen, in 1969, that I realised I was gay. And in my hometown of Melbourne there were no LGBT+ rights organisations. Not even any helplines or counselling services. There was absolutely nothing. Homosexuality was a serious criminal offence, which could be punishable by several years' imprisonment, and even enforced psychiatric treatment. Gay bashing was the norm, often perpetrated by the police with impunity. So I had no model about what LGBT+ people could do to challenge our oppression.

I knew and accepted that I was gay amazingly quickly, given my deeply fundamentalist Christian upbringing. After falling in love with a man for the first time and beginning our relationship, I remember thinking to myself, *How can this be wrong? No one is being harmed. This gives both me and him immense emotional fulfilment.* For me, the reality of being gay blew away all the dogma about it being wrong. I realised that when it comes to Christian teaching, Jesus Christ reportedly condemned many sins, but he never once condemned homosexuality. All those damnations were from St Paul (who was a mere mortal), or were way back in the Old Testament. Moreover, the Old Testament also said all kinds of other things, like you must not wear garments with mixed fibres. It's a sin to eat shellfish. Men must not trim the corners of their beards. Yet no Christians in the twentieth century were demanding adherence to those biblical laws and expectations.

So, having no template of my own, I looked to the Black civil rights movement. I thought to myself, *They've shown what LGBT+ people need to do. What they've done to win their rights, we must do to win ours.* I reasoned in my own mind that if Black people are an oppressed minority, then so too are LGBT+ people. And if Black people have a claim for equality and social justice, then so do we, who are LGBT+.

I remember reading, in the latter part of 1969, about a march in New York by gay people demanding civil rights. It was only a little 'news in brief' – no more than thirty words. But I remember those words so very clearly. I thought, *Yes, I want to be part of that. I want to make my contribution towards the liberation of LGBT+ people.* So I began to study even more closely the history of how the Black civil rights movement overturned segregation in the Deep South, and how they won voting rights.

It was very clear to me that we LGBTs were up against incredible hostility from the law and every social institution. Pleading for LGBT+ rights probably wouldn't work; neither would traditional lobbying. We would have to use the same Gandhian tactics of nonviolent direct action and civil disobedience as the Black civil rights movement had done. It would require similar sacrifice, courage and determination. We'd have to use protest to pressure an intransigent, ignorant and indifferent society to acknowledge our existence and our right to equality.

Initially I tried to lobby Members of Parliament. I wrote letters to newspapers. They were all ignored. It was impossible to get anyone in the Establishment in late-1960s Australia to take LGBT+ rights seriously. I can remember thinking to myself, *Boy, this is going to be a long, hard struggle. We are up against the homophobia, biphobia and transphobia, not just of decades or centuries, but of millennia.*

The consensus, historically and contemporarily, was that LGBTs were mad, bad and sad. Being gay was deemed immoral, criminal and unnatural. That was the dominant view. I knew to overturn this prejudice would take a huge, protracted struggle. Looking at the experience of the Black civil rights movement, I calculated that it would probably take about fifty years in Western countries like Australia, the United States and Britain to overturn legal inequality and discrimination – and to change public attitudes.

So I was in it for the long haul. But I never intended to make this my life's work. I began my activism part time in the evenings, and occasionally at weekends. I would write letters to newspapers. I tried to interest and engage other gay people who I met through semi-underground gay friendship and party networks. I recall proposing to them the idea of setting up an LGBT+ rights group in Melbourne in late 1969, when no such a group had even been conceived, let alone existed. I was stung by their responses. These were mostly older gay men.

'Go away, what do you know?'

'You're only seventeen; you'll get us all arrested.'

There was no recognition that we LGBTs had a claim for justice, just a strong fear of what might happen if we organised and campaigned. Apart from my partner, no one seemed to believe that we could fight for and *win* our rights, just like the Black civil rights movement in America had done.

I was inspired by hearing that one of the leaders of the Black Power movement in the US, Huey Newton, had in 1969 declared that gay liberation was a legitimate part of the struggle for the liberation of humanity. His declaration was extraordinary, given the level of homophobia in sections of the African American community at the time. But Huey was absolutely clear. Black people were part of a wider, broader struggle, and this included the movements for women's liberation and gay liberation. My thinking exactly. If we all worked together, stood together and supported each other, we would collectively be stronger.

When I came to London in 1971, aged nineteen, I joined the newly formed Gay Liberation Front (GLF), which was the first real mass movement of LGBT+ people in Britain. It was the first time ever that not dozens, not hundreds, but *thousands* of LGBT+ people came out. The weekly GLF meetings had sometimes 300–500 people in attendance. There were no leaders. It was a grassroots, non-hierarchical, democratic movement. We took on the government, police, Church, media and medical profession. GLF was also allied with other social movements. When the Black activists known as the Mangrove Nine were facing trial on trumped-up charges, GLF was one of the few non-Black organisations to stand in solidarity with them. Likewise, when the women's liberation movement held a mass rally against the sexism and misogyny of the Miss World contest in 1971, GLF was there with them.

GLF wasn't just about equality. In fact, it wasn't really about equality at all. I don't think the word 'equality' ever passed the lips of those of us in GLF. We wanted liberation, not mere equal rights within the flawed status quo. Our goal was the transformation of society to create a new sexual democracy for everyone, LGBT+ and straight. We challenged puritanism, erotophobia and misogyny, as well as homophobia, biphobia and transphobia. Our strategy was to join forces with everybody else who also wanted social change. So in 1971, GLF marched with trade unions against the Industrial Relations Bill, to support workers' rights. We showed similar solidarity with Greeks fighting the colonels' junta, Spaniards resisting Franco and the civil rights movement in the north of Ireland.

So anyway, to get to the story of my song... 'To Be Young, Gifted and Black'. I first heard it in late 1970 or early 1971. It had been released on Nina Simone's album *Black Gold* not long before. I immediately saw it as an incredibly proud, positive affirmation of Black identity and culture, which of course I supported. But it also spoke to me as a young gay man. I imagined the rewording of those lyrics as talking about LGBT+ people: how we were young, gifted and gay. And like Black people, despite all the prejudice and hate thrown at us, we were also proud and determined to stand up for our liberation and freedom. I found this song incredibly uplifting and powerful, emotionally and politically. Sure, there were many other great civil rights songs that inspired me and which I embraced. But this song really struck a special note. It was saying to the younger generation of Black people, *Be proud. A better future is possible. You are talented and worthwhile. You can be change-makers.* I saw the song's core principles of pride and upliftment as being translatable to young LGBTs as well.

Nina Simone was a great songstress of the civil rights movement and a great activist herself. She spoke and sang at many rallies during the 1960s to support the struggle for African American emancipation. I'm immensely grateful that 'To Be Young, Gifted and Black' indirectly helped inspire my own early LGBT+ self-affirmation and human rights activism.

'To Be Young, Gifted and Black'
Written by Nina Simone and Weldon Irvine
Performed by Nina Simone
Taken from the album *Black Gold*, released on RCA Records in
1969

Apple Music   Spotify

This story was first performed at Wilton's Music Hall on 9 August 2017.

Peter Tatchell has been campaigning on issues of human rights, democracy, LGBT+ freedom and global justice since 1967, and his campaigns have led to tangible changes in international law, including the UK 2010 Equality Act and the 2013 Same Sex Marriage Act. He lives in London.

Part 2 – Belonging

Prasanna Puwanarajah

When I was asked to talk about a song that changed my life, I immediately knew the answer to the question.

Straight away I thought about a Scots song by the poet, intellectual, activist and songwriter Hamish Henderson, called 'Freedom Come All Ye', written in 1960.

The version of the song that I want to share with you is a live version, sung a cappella by Karine Polwart in the Italian Chapel in Lamb Holm in Orkney, and recorded by Andy Crabb as part of Cape Farewell's Sea Change project, in which artists of all denominations explored the landscape, history and art of Orkney.

I heard this recording for the first time in 2015, around the time of the Scottish independence referendum, when a friend of mine played it for me. And it went through me like a cold wind.

While following the coverage of the referendum from the relative distance of England, I'd found myself experiencing a desire, a yearning, to explore and fill a gap that had long troubled me. Because, whereas I had never known how to describe myself – even *to* myself – here, on the TV, were brown people saying, simply, 'I'm Scottish.' Not qualifying it as 'Scottish Asian'. Just, 'I'm Scottish.' And rejoicing in that. In that being who they were.

And I felt so jealous of them, I cannot even find the words to describe it.

As you might be able to tell from my name, I am Sri Lankan Tamil, East Anglian, south-coast English – which, on the census form, falls under 'Any Other Asian, Please Describe'.

I've been asked to describe my heritage my whole life, with varying success. My name is a slayer of primary school register-takers. Someone recently said, 'Ah yes, once you hear the name Prasanna Puwan-Jara, you never forget it,' unaware that they'd mangled the pronounciation of my name in the process.

What I remember is being bullied on the way home from secondary school for wearing an England football shirt.

So... not English...

Not English Asian...

Not *really* Asian...

Not British Asian...

Just me.

And given that, for me, identity is an act of community and plurality as much as it's about the self, 'just me' was far too small a group. It's an insignificant, nervous, nation of one.

My friend, the actor and poet/musician Riz Ahmed, is so much more eloquent than I am on this subject, so I'm going to nick some words from him to try and articulate the disconnect in me when I tell you that I've looked in the mirror my whole life, and I've seen not a man, but a brown man.

'Here we are,' says Riz, 'the bastard children of modern Britain. You're not quite fully accepted into the family, into the nation's self-image. There's a heartbreak around that feeling, an anger. It's similar to feeling like a jilted lover – you have a right to be in the room, to partake, but by dint of your birth, you're excluded. You're not considered to be the proper thing.' That's Riz.

And he's right. For me, being a brown boy who used to wish that he was white, who now feels quite a lot of guilt for feeling that but hasn't quite replaced that guilt with anything else, and whose ownership of self feels like a shifting mosaic of colonisation from the outside and belligerence from within, the idea of belonging is complicated. I had wanted so badly, and for so long, to be in the presence of something – anything – be it a song, a poem, a word, a view – that would so completely and roundly speak for me, and to me, to my core, to every twist of my genome and self, and show me who I might be.

And then along came this song.

Henderson himself described it as 'expressing my hopes for Scotland, and the survival of humanity on this beleaguered planet'. It is luminous, profound but quite unromantic. It speaks for Scotland as a nation and for a nation of people from everywhere.

It's about a country that is part of a union that has a dark colonial past – a past that, outside of songs like this, we are not talking about.

And we need to, badly.

What have we done to broken families in lands we've harried?

What's been done to us?

What have we been made to do?

How do we reconcile?

How do we hold anyone or anything to account?

How do we mourn?

How do we self-determine?

It strikes me that these are all questions about Sri Lanka as much as they are questions about Scotland – or about anywhere, in any time.

But above all, this song hopes for a better, warless world, which it conjures up itself. That world is equal. Peace is everywhere.

It belongs to everyone. It's a world where the greatest act of self-determination is the freedom to love whoever you love. To be whoever you are.

So, in the midst of the Scottish independence referendum, I listened to this beautiful song and wished I was Scottish. Or more specifically, wished I was part of anything so radiantly hopeful.

This song was a window into a feeling that I'd yearned for my whole life. As, I suspect, have many of you reading this.

And, as Riz says, I think it's a feeling that is like love.

I listen to this song regularly, and it returns me to that feeling. It's the feeling of not being jilted, of being accepted.

Karine Polwart sang this in a chapel, which I've visited, on Lamb Holm in Orkney. The winds that you will hear before her gorgeous, timeless, beautiful, exposed performance are the same Orcadian winds that this brown boy has felt on his skin.

My mum comes from a breezy island off the coast of Sri Lanka. So I think that there's more that connects us than divides us, if we hope for that to be true.

'Freedom Come All Ye'
Written by Hamish Henderson
Performed by Karine Polwart in the Italian Chapel, Orkney in
August 2013 as part of Cape Farewell's Sea Change project
https://vimeo.com/73406037

Vimeo

This story was performed at Wilton's Music Hall on 30 May 2016.

Prasanna Puwanarajah studied medicine at New College, Oxford, before embarking on a hugely successful career in the arts. He is known as an actor (*Line of Duty*, *Doctor Foster*, *Patrick Melrose*), a playwright (*Nightwatchman*) and a director for stage (*Moth*, *The Reluctant Fundamentalist*) and screen (*Ballywalter*). He is a trustee of the National Youth Theatre, an artistic associate at the Donmar Warehouse and a patron of the Theatrical Guild.

Ingrid Oliver

It all started when an ex-boyfriend of mine told me I should probably start exercising more.

What he said was, 'I just want you to be healthier, babe, for you.'

What I heard was, 'I just want you to be thinner, babe, for me.'

So I dumped him.

I actually didn't dump him at that point. I did eventually – obviously, that's why he's an ex. But not for that. Because actually, he had a point. He was worried about my health.

God, I'm really justifying this. Clearly, I'm still not over him.

At the time I was in a double act with my best friend, Lorna. We were writing a lot. In fact, writing was our full-time job. We'd written three Edinburgh shows, two pilots, two series for the BBC, all in the space of about five years. That was a lot of writing. And the way we liked to work was to sit in her living room eating a lot of Percy Pigs, and those M&S crisps, the posh ones that are all different shapes, tapping out sketches on our thirteen-inch MacBook Airs. And when we had done a full day's work, we'd celebrate with a bottle of Prosecco. Each.

So inevitably, the weight had crept up, and my ex had been right. I wasn't healthy. And it wasn't just about the weight gain.

(Although, spoiler alert, it was definitely also about the weight gain).

I also had a twenty- to thirty-a-day a cigarette habit. I drank too much. Like most writers, I spent all day inside my own head, rarely venturing out for fresh air or exercise. I thought it was kind of romantic. I imagined I was very much like a Byron or a Keats, if Byron or Keats had written catchphrase comedy for BBC Three online.

But the reality was my knees had started to buckle every time I walked up a flight of stairs. Which was not good. And when I got to the top, it sounded like I was having a full-blown asthma attack. I knew at that point that I had to do something.

So I joined my local council gym. I figured a group activity would keep me more motivated than doing something on my own. I searched through their class timetable, immediately discounting anything that had the words 'high intensity' or 'pump', because I'm not mental. And my eye was drawn towards Zumba.

Now, for those of you that don't know (although I can't imagine anyone doesn't know) a Zumba class is basically aerobics set to Latin music, and I figured that anything that involves dancing could surely not be that bad. And I was right. I absolutely loved it immediately. Before Zumba – or BZ, as I came to think of it – whenever I complained about going to the gym, annoying people would always say, 'Oh, you just haven't found your thing yet.' And I thought, I will never have a *thing*. What kind of pervert has a *thing* for exercise? But I was wrong, and they were right, which is always annoying. I had found my thing. And after that first class, I immediately went out and I bought a couple of sports bras and some activewear. That's how you know it's serious. And my boyfriend was very impressed. I started going once, twice, three times a week and would miss it on the days when there was no class. Even when I was hung over I would drag myself out of bed, forgo my beloved first cigarette of the day and head over to the leisure centre. I loved the music, which wasn't just salsa, but a mixture of Latin, African and Arabic beats, R & B, pop and hip-hop, the diversity of the music reflecting the diversity of us, the dancers, people (mainly women) from Jamaica, Nigeria, Turkey, China, Japan, Thailand, Saudi Arabia, Germany.

I came to depend on my Zumba class. And I know that people say that exercise releases endorphins. But it was more than that. There was something about standing in a room full of women, first thing in the morning, dancing to Shakira, that felt important. There was nowhere to hide in our class, because everyone faced a huge mirror at the front. You could see everyone at all times. And when you see people day in, day out, you come to recognise changes in their faces. You know if they're having a good day or a bad day. When I eventually broke up with my boyfriend (Yay!) I was drinking and I was smoking too much, but I was also still turning up to class. And at the sight of my ashen face, these women would wordlessly squeeze my shoulder in between 'Hips Don't Lie' and 'Take on Me'. They would mouth, 'Are you OK?' into the mirror. I was grateful for them, and I was reminded of what a wonderful thing it is to be a woman; to be part of a sisterhood of mothers and aunts and grandmothers.

That's not to say that men aren't welcome at Zumba – quite the opposite. We've had several men join the class over the years. The most unlikely of them is a very softly spoken man in his late sixties. Even more unlikely is the fact that he is Sir Oswald Mosley's grandson. (I'm not gonna lie; it really tickles me to think of how much a big old racist like Mosley would have hated the idea of his grandson shaking his booty to foreign music in a room full of first-, second- and third-generation immigrants. Welcome to south-east London, bitch.)

I've tried to work out why *this* Zumba class is so special. Why it means so much to me. Because it is. And it does. Whenever I go anywhere else, if a job takes me to another city, I will always seek out the nearest Zumba class. And it's never as good. And I know it's partly because of the amazing women in it, but it is also mainly because of one amazing woman: the one who stands at the front of the room. The one who teaches us the steps, the one who chooses which tracks to play. Her name is Topaz White. *Topaz White!* Even her name makes her sound like some sort of cool shaman! And in some ways, that's exactly what she is. She performs some kind of weird voodoo every Monday, Wednesday and Friday at 10 a.m. Because no matter how you're feeling when you walk into that room, you leave feeling better. And she is kind and encouraging and inspiring and lives to give others energy, even when occasionally she herself has none, and frankly we don't deserve her.

The song that I'd say most sums up what all of this means to me is 'Proud Mary'. It's a class favourite. And I can always tell how fit I am by whether or not I can do the whole routine carrying weights. (At the moment I can't, and it's really pissing me off...) Whenever I hear this song at a party or in a bar, I have to get up and do the routine. I've taught many people the 'Proud Mary' dance – it's like a little gift I like to give to them, often against their will. There was a time I moved to LA for a year and it came on at a swanky showbiz party, and I was so homesick for London and my Zumba class that I actually cried, and I forced – and I do mean forced – a Hollywood actor to do the routine with me. (He bloody loved it.)

Now this version of the song is sung by, of course, Tina Turner, who at the time was famously stuck in an abusive relationship with her partner. So I think of it as a survivor's song, about someone who's turned their back on misery and found redemption through music. And that is how I feel about our Zumba class. It's where we go, week in, week out, just to shake it off (in the words of Taylor Swift). Over the last six years, as a group, we've had seventeen break-ups – three of those were mine (not even joking) – four cancer diagnoses and one death. And we've always come out the other side dancing. And I can't tell you how joyous is to stand in a room full of people who smile and laugh and clap every time they hear the opening bars to this song. I mean, there are also groans, because it's really fucking knackering. But it still has that same glorious effect, even though we have danced to it three times a week, every week, for the last six bloody years.

There's a point in the song when the drums kick in, we're all dancing and throwing our arms in the air and I tell you, it is the closest thing I've ever come to genuine euphoria, and I highly recommend it.

'Proud Mary'
Written by John Fogerty
Performed by Ike and Tina Turner
Taken from the album *Workin' Together*, released on Capitol
Records in 1970

Apple Music   Spotify

This story was first performed at Wilton's Music Hall on 12 October 2019.

Ingrid Oliver is a comedian, writer and actress. As part of the double act Watson and Oliver, she's performed at the Edinburgh Fringe festival and in her own BBC Three sketch comedy series. She's also appeared in *Doctor Who*, and in 2013 was named star baker in an episode of the *Great Comic Relief Bake Off*.

Haresh Patel

The song that changed my life is the one that woke me up to the *sound* of music.

It's a song from the eighties, and it's both a timeless classic and thoroughly dated. Like me.

Growing up, I had the best parents a child could wish for: Television and Radio. Saturday morning kids' TV, *Top of the Pops* and MTV. The exotic videos with their machine worlds and glitter; all these guitars, power ballads, soaring vocals. They were faraway and impossible worlds to escape to.

The sound of the eighties was the sound of machines in music, spiky blankets of synthesisers and samplers, of digital recording and digital reverbs.

While I was at secondary school, A-ha released the much-hyped video for their song 'Take on Me'. They'd spent a lot of money on it – something like £100k, which was huge at the time. Hype is hype, of course, and it felt to me as though amazing things were happening every week during that time, but MTV really made a lot of noise about this video, so understandably I was excited.

When the time came, I sat right in front of my TV. The drums started up, the pencil-drawing comic strip began to animate. And as that famous keyboard riff came in, it was like a cold spoon of electric ice cream going straight into my brain.

Watching that video was the first time that teenaged me realised the magical power of creativity. *Someone* had created this animation with nothing more than a pencil and some paper! I had a pencil and some paper! Maybe I could create something like this too?

It had never really sunk in until that moment that I could actually make music and art myself. There was something about escaping – literally – into a comic book that really struck a chord with me.

Of course, the song went on to be a huge worldwide hit and, unsurprisingly, a lot of my schoolfriends saw the video. We had a Yamaha DX7 at school – the very same keyboard the band used in the song – and that keyboard riff was hammered out endlessly, really badly, by all of us, every time the teacher wasn't around. It was a badge of honour if you could play it without messing it up. I cracked it a few times, and that satisfaction lasted for hours.

Being a schoolboy at the time, I couldn't afford to buy much music, so, like many of my contemporaries, I recorded my favourite songs off the radio, waiting for the chart rundown and hoping that the DJ would not talk over the intro. (They always did, though. *So* annoying).

A-ha's first album came out the following year. I'd already heard – and loved – their subsequent singles 'Sun Always Shines' and 'Train of Thought', so I saved up and bought it on cassette. I still remember the new-plastic smell of the packaging, the moody photography on the cover and every sound on every song. I listened to it all again and again, devoting a deep and serious study to it. I obsessed about every choice of note, every guitar lick, every vocal, tried to find the meaning in everything. Like teenagers do.

Back in those pre-internet days, *Smash Hits* and *Just 17* were our bibles, pop-centric music magazines, filled with gossip, lyrics and more. The girls at school would pore over the pictures, while I'd pore over the lyrics, looking for clues into the bands' inner secrets. From those magazines, I discovered that A-ha been influenced by the Beatles, Echo and the Bunnymen and the Doors. The first two I'd heard of, but the Doors were new to me, and that discovery opened up another avenue for exploration.

My love of A-ha even inspired me to start my own pop band with a fellow fan from school. I learned to play the guitar, while he sang. My obsession with the way the songs were constructed led me to save up and buy a little home studio, consisting of a drum machine, a cheap synthesiser and a reverb unit. The reverb unit was crucial, as A-ha's sound was soaked in reverbs that made the vocals soar like mountains.

But those were all the buttons and gadgets that I could afford. Nevertheless, it was a brilliant education, making music and shaping sounds, and managing the tiny technical capabilities of a four-track set-up while trying to get as big a sound as possible.

Eventually, I got good enough at it to start working with other acts, and somehow ended up graduating to proper studios, with loud hairy heavy-metal groups. (They didn't like A-ha as much as I did. I had to keep that bit quiet.)

Nowadays, of course, 'Take on Me' has become a piece of pop-culture history, a karaoke classic, a wedding-band standard. I moved on too, and I slowly began to file A-ha away on my own musical shelf. It wasn't so much that I was embarrassed. It was just that I'd discovered a wealth of new listening pleasures.

But that teenage obsession is still with me today. I work as a sound designer for film and TV, and that kind of deep listening is still my favourite thing to do in the whole world. I can do it anywhere.

Perhaps it's surprising that after all these years, 'Take on Me' would be my musical North Star. The most amazing thing about great songs is that they say what you can't. They can give you a voice when you lose your own.

Recorded music is emotional time travel. When I listen to 'Take on Me' nowadays, it sounds like a song sent from my younger self to my older self. It's a reminder to let my youthful side in. It also connects me to my daughter – she loves the song as well – and it reminds me to have as much fun with her as I possibly can.

Like the character in the song, I sometimes feel as though I've stumbled through life and made a few poor choices along the way. And I've definitely not taken as many chances as I should have. I've played it safe in many ways, and often not let people take chances on me.

But what I've learned in telling this story – first on stage and now in this book – is that in the end it's no better to be safe than sorry.

'Take on Me'
Written by Magne Furuholmen, Morten Harket and Pål Waaktar
Performed by A-ha
Taken from the album *MTV Unplugged: Summer Solstice*, released
on Polydor Records in 2017

Apple Music

Spotify

This story was first performed for *OneTrackMinds* Hidden Tracks
at Omeara London on 14 January 2019.

Haresh Patel is a London-based sound recordist and sound
designer for films, commercials, music and bespoke audio. To him,
sounds, vibrations and music are the fundamental structure of life,
the universe and everything. He also likes cake way too much, but
he is working on that.

Rhik Samadder

'The greatest mystery is not that we've been flung at random between this profusion of matter and the stars. But that from this prison we can draw from ourselves images powerful enough to deny our nothingness.'

The words of Geri Halliwell on leaving the Spice Girls. She knew she would be disappointing a great many people. I'd like to write about disappointment as my theme for this story, and I can only apologise for that.

I know disappointment is not one of the big themes. It's not the thrill of first love or finding your calling.

Disappointment is not like that.

Disappointment is what happens when life refuses to cast you in a story you have written for yourself.

I was looking for a story when I was fourteen. Picture a sort of never-been-kissed twiglet of a thing who, more than stories in fact, was looking for friendship. I was alone. I was lonely. And I thought that music could help me find what I was looking for. I remember I went up to the most popular boy in our year – Aiden, his name was – and I asked him to make me a mix tape of cool music that cool people liked that would make me cool and popular. And to his credit, he came back a few days later and he had this cassette tape. And it had an acid smiley face on it, with the words 'Happy Hardcore' written across it in felt tip.

I listened to ninety minutes of what I can only describe as psychopathically intense dance music. And I had three thoughts. I thought to myself:

1) This is what popular music is.
2) I hate it.
3) I will have to pretend to like this for the rest of my life.

Luckily, of course, that didn't happen. In fact, my dream came true – I was befriended, some time after all this, by two older boys in my school. And they were kind of amazing. They were older. They were a lot taller. One of them – Martin – was six foot seven, which was a whole foot taller than me. We'd walk around looking like Prince and his bodyguards. I loved hanging out with them, and they introduced me to so many things. They introduced me to writers like André Malraux, who I quoted at the top of this piece (that was not Geri Halliwell, that was a lie), but they also introduced me to a lot of music.

Martin would make me these mix tapes, but these ones had beautiful liner notes with very small, neat handwriting about all the songs. That was the sort of currency of boys back then.

The mix tapes were amazing. They had Gang of Four, Miles Davis, Dylan, Jimi. But there was one song by Joni Mitchell that changed everything for me.

It's a song called 'Amelia', and not many people know it. Even Joni Mitchell fans. Basically it's about Joni driving across this desert following a failed love affair. And she's having this imaginary dialogue with Amelia Earhart, the great aviator who disappeared over the Pacific as if lost to the air itself.

And it's about the cost of ambition, especially for women. It's about the limits of love. It's about that lonely place within us all that we can never outrun. And it's about disappointment. The closest it comes to a chorus is Joni repeatedly consoling Amelia – or I guess herself – that everything she's experienced to that point has been a series of false alarms.

It was the most beautiful thing I had ever heard. I could feel my brain expanding – physically feel that, as if it was trying to get a grasp on this strange new thing.

It was so beautiful. But it was not only beautiful – it taught me something *about* beauty. It seemed to suggest that because beauty *that* sublime could come from loss, from things that didn't work out, that was *itself* a source of beauty. And that's a strange idea. It doesn't make much sense, really, on the surface. But then I realised that if that's true, then maybe beauty is not located in the stories that we want to tell, it's somewhere else. Maybe it began once we stopped talking.

It also suggested that André Malraux was wrong. I think beauty *is* in those powerful images. But they don't help us deny our nothingness: they help to accept it and keep living. And this song has really done that for me throughout my life.

I remember thinking that love would banish that lonely place. But it doesn't. I remember finding a calling – I was acting, but I had to give it up, as I couldn't make it work. And then I tried to set down some beauty of my own. I wrote a book, and it did well, and I was prouder of that than anything I've ever done. And one day shortly after that, I woke up. And I was still myself. Nothing had transformed magically. But that was OK.

There is a strange coda to this story. Those two boys I mentioned. We hadn't seen each other for a long, long time. We fell out. I can't remember what it was about, but it must have been bad. We just stopped talking. And after my book came out, Martin got in touch again. He wanted to apologise. He said that he was sorry for those mix tapes that he had made, because he felt that in some way he was trying to impose his taste on me and it wasn't right. He also said that the last time we had seen each other, he had poured a drink over me. And he had carried this for twenty years and he couldn't live with himself. The guilt of it, he said – he thought he'd scarred me for life.

The thing is, I couldn't remember that. He'd been carrying this around. This was his own false alarm. Joni Mitchell in the song keeps talking about false alarms. And this was his false alarm. I was fine. I couldn't even remember it. Those tapes. I messaged him. They saved me. They were a rope thrown down a well.

'Amelia'
Written by Joni Mitchell
Performed by Joni Mitchell
Taken from the album *Hejira*, released on Asylum Records in 1976

Apple Music   Spotify

This story was first performed at Wilton's Music Hall on 11 October 2019.

Rhik Samadder is an actor, columnist, broadcaster and author. He created the cult food column 'Inspect a Gadget' for the *Guardian* newspaper, which has been featured internationally. He presented *How to Retire at 40* on Channel 4, and has appeared on Radio 4's *Today* Programme, Sky News and Radio 5 Live, among others. He has been a guest on many podcasts, including the number-one-rated *The High Low*. As an actor, his credits include the lead role in *The Indian Boy* at the RSC, as well as appearances on BBC, HBO, ITV and others. His memoir *I Never Said I Loved You*, released in August 2019, became a *Sunday Times* bestseller. He lives in London.

Andy Nyman

The year is 1982. The place is Leicester.

Already this is a sexy story.

I was sixteen, and there was something happening in England that was truly revolutionary. Something that scared the government to such a degree that it created fear and panic, and brought about some extraordinary actions.

The home-video explosion was in full bloom, and it was massive. Suddenly we weren't just limited to the three (only three!) channels that we had to watch. If you wanted to see *Raiders of the Lost Ark*, you didn't have to wait until Christmas any more and hope that it was on, because now there were video-rental shops.

These places had thousands and thousands of videos. And it was amazing. It was an amazing explosion that seemed to change everything. It went mad. Very soon, one in three homes in Britain had a video machine. And suddenly every newsagent, garage and sweet shop was a video club.

And next to *The Sting*, *Towering Inferno* and many other family-friendly favourites, was the part of the video club that I loved the most – the horror section.

Now, these were not the cosy Hammer Horrors, or Universal

Dracula/Frankenstein/Wolf Man horror films that BBC Two showed in their famous double bills at the time. This was a new breed of titles from around the world, and to a horror-hungry sixteen-year-old like me, these new titles presented an entirely new challenge that seemed to say, 'Dare you watch me?'

To which I would reply, 'Yes. Absolutely.'

Zombie Flesh-Eaters, Texas Chainsaw Massacre, Night of the Living Dead, Driller Killer, House by the Cemetery, I Spit on Your Grave. These were the good ones. You see, what blew my mind was that, in among these titles, these videos with their ridiculous and outrageously lurid covers, was the work of some genuinely incredible directors.

Not all of them, I should say – I sat through some absolute fucking shit – but the good ones were absolutely amazing. Because the directors that were making the good ones were people that we'd never heard of. And they were people of genuine and extraordinary talent. Mario Bava, Wes Craven, Tobe Hooper, Lucio Fulci, to name just a few.

Now, my favourite video shop was in my local garage. It had an amazing collection of videos. What was most extraordinary was the man who ran it. It was impossible to determine where this man came from. He could have been Russian, Indian, Chinese – you just could not work it out. He was about six foot four, with dark olive skin, piercing blue eyes, a massive beard and a bizarre grin that never left his face. No matter what you would rent, he would always say the same thing – 'One pound ninety-nine!' – followed by a raucous, genial laugh.

I called him Rasputin. And he was known as Rasputin to all of our friends and my family. You would often hear my dad saying, 'You're not going to bloody Rasputin's till you've done your homework.'

I rented many, many, many films from Rasputin's. I was down there all the time. Some were good. Some were absolutely awful. But there was one that changed my life in the autumn of 1982.

I went into Rasputin's, I looked on the shelf, and I spotted a video cover that I had never seen before. There it was. *Deep Red* by Dario Argento. The front cover had David Hemmings holding a torch, looking through a smashed window. It was a pretty unremarkable cover. But down in the bottom left was a sticker that said: CAUTION: CONTAINS EXTREME BLOODY VIOLENCE!

Now I *adore* the use of the word 'caution' on that sticker, because we all know it's actually saying: 'Rent this fucker! It's really brutal!'

It was the ultimate challenge. So with a swift £1.99 I rented *Deep Red* and took it home.

I had no idea what I'd let myself in for.

I sat in our front room. I pressed play on the video.

What I didn't realise at the time was that *Deep Red* is director Dario Argento's masterpiece. It's a very particular type of violent Italian whodunnit known as the giallo because the books they were based on were printed on yellow paper, or *giallo* in Italian. And *Deep Red* is the greatest *giallo* ever made. The look of it, the style of it, the violence of it. I've never seen anything like it. The final revelation of the killer – which I will not spoil for you here – blew my mind.

The magic trick that this film played on me was unreal. The sheer chutzpah of it was astonishing. It's a truly brilliant film, and I urge you to see it if you haven't already done so.

But the icing on the cake – the thing that made the film so extraordinarily, so utterly, remarkably, insanely original – was the soundtrack.

Dario Argento had collaborated with Ennio Morricone on all of his other films. But they'd had a massive falling-out on their final collaboration, Argento's film *Four Flies on Grey Velvet* – which is also amazing, but insane.

So Argento asked another composer, a jazz pianist called Giorgio Gaslini, to compose music for *Deep Red*. Argento heard the first couple of things that Gaslini composed and he hated them. He fired him. It wasn't what was in Argento's head at all.

So then he got on a plane and he came to London and he asked Pink Floyd if they would compose the music for *Deep Red*. They had absolutely no interest in doing so. (They had probably seen *Four Flies on Grey Velvet*).

So he went back to Italy and he stumbled across a demo tape for an Italian prog rock group called Goblin. And the second he heard that demo tape, he knew he'd found it. The music for his film.

There I was, sat in our front room. And I pressed play. And the second I heard this music, I knew all bets were off. There was no safe ground.

I'd never heard anything like it. The music completely shook me.

Its mental, pumping, neo-gothic sound was unlike anything that I'd heard before, and it had a dramatic impact on me. So strong was that impact that twenty-eight years later, when Jeremy Dyson and I were putting on our play *Ghost Stories*, we chose that song as our theme music. Night after night I would watch as that music had the same impact on a West End audience that it had on me in 1982.

It shook them.

About three months after I first rented *Deep Red*, the Department of Public Prosecutions published its infamous video nasties list. On that list were seventy-two film titles that the Department of Public Prosecutions called 'obscene' and decided needed to be seized.

Amazingly, this led to police storming into the video clubs, garages, shops and newsagents that had been stocking these films, which had all been legally purchased, and seizing them – and by seizing them, I mean they would pull them off the shelves and put them into bin bags. They also took any other films that they decided they didn't like the look of, even if they weren't on the list.

Once the bin bags were sealed, they were sent away and destroyed. And all of those videos were burned in an incinerator.

Now this is an act tantamount to book burning. It's comparable to what they did in Nazi Germany or in the Deep South.

When I went back to Rasputin's next, the horror section had gone and Rasputin's beaming grin wasn't quite as strong as it had been. It felt like the beginning of the end.

When I was working on writing this, it really made me think about that period of our recent history. Within the madness, the Wild West-ness of the home-video explosion, something remarkable really did happen. A generation had a flash-burn experience. We were given a little taste of something subversive, something that really shook the core of Britain. That really scared those who governed us.

Now, I love that I lived through that period. It had a profound effect on me, and it's shaped the work that I've gone on to create.

I always get a buzz whenever I play this song. Part of that is because I still get excited by the film, and by my memories of that time. But I think part of it is also a little buzz of fear about what I feel I *really* saw back then. I saw how quickly society can change, how it can legitimise taking, stealing or destroying something just because it doesn't understand it. And it does it all under the cloak of lawfulness and protection.

And that really is something to be scared of.

'Profondo Rosso' (Deep Red)
Written by Massimo Morante, Maurizio Guarini, Fabio Pignatelli
and Agostino Marangolo
Performed by Goblin
Taken from the 1975 soundtrack album to the film *Deep Red*,
released on Cinevox

Apple Music   Spotify

This story was first told at Wilton's Music Hall on 15 February 2018.

Andy Nyman is an actor, writer and director. He's appeared in countless films and TV series, including *Severance*, *Kick Ass 2*, *Peaky Blinders*, *Dead Set* and *Crooked House*. On stage, he starred as Tevye in *Fiddler on the Roof* and created the box-office hit *Ghost Stories*, which was turned into a film in 2017. He is a frequent collaborator of magician and mentalist Derren Brown, and co-wrote and co-directed four of his stage shows.

Part 3 – Beloving

Rosa Dachtler

I wrote the first draft of this story on a beautiful Sunday last summer. I poured a full first draft onto the page without really thinking, and, naturally, it was a mess. I stopped for a mental reset, made cup of coffee number four and realised it was Father's Day.

The truth is, I can never remember when Mother's Day or Father's Day are. Maybe it's one of the casualties of growing up in two countries. You develop zero built-in understanding of national holidays. And it doesn't help if your parents are so committed to rejecting social norms that they actively give up on the two days a year that are, in theory, all about them. But even though my folks didn't acknowledge the sacred or social aspects of Easter or Shrove Tuesday, they were practical enough to at least involve the food. We always had some kind of pre-hibernation winter feast in lieu of a Christmas dinner and, when your mom is from Holland, every Tuesday can be Pancake Tuesday. So, in honour of that practicality, I'd like to dedicate this story to my parents.

They are both, in their own ways, story people. My mom is a radio DJ and my dad is a musician, and I've inherited this idea from them that music is where human beings find their voice for the stories we don't know how to tell. Mind you, they also both love telling stories. Once, my dad performed in a small village and the sound failed mid-set. The sound! So, naturally, he kept people entertained with a made-up history of the town – somehow without offending any of the locals...

What I'm about to tell you is a story about stories. It's also a story about family, which is one of the reasons I've never told it to anyone before. Usually, when I talk about my family in detail, I talk about the big deals – unusual things like being homeschooled in America. Or broken things, like being homeschooled in America.

I think I do this because they are interesting and entertaining things to talk about, but also because I like to understand my own story by telling people I trust about the parts that I can't make sense of. They become mirrors of my experience. We exchange tales about life and family. We react to what we're hearing and share our understanding. Hopefully we come away with perspective, knowing each other and even knowing ourselves a little bit better.

When I was invited to contribute a story to *OneTrackMinds*, I searched and searched for the right one. I looked at all my big deals, at all the crises, all the weirdness. Music illuminates every part of my life, but nothing called out to me, none of my usual stories felt right. When I finally landed on this story, I realised it was something I hadn't thought about for years, something clear but not present. Telling you this is a selfish exercise, really, because if I'm lucky it will help me better understand an experience I've never shared.

When I was eight years old, living in Bath, I was vaguely aware that my parents were working very hard on immigration paperwork. Although I didn't know the details, I did know that the Nintendo 64 my brother and I loved would not follow us to the new country. I knew that having my own room was a temporary luxury I wouldn't be able to enjoy across the ocean. I did not know that my voice, my mannerisms, even my sense of humour were about to change profoundly, and that by the time I reached the age of twenty-seven I'd sound like a Canadian raised on Radio 4. For the record, I was born in Amsterdam and spent my first nine years in Britain and my second nine in the United States. And I do like Radio 4. I've been back in the UK for nearly a decade now. But when people ask me, 'So, like, are you Dutch or American or British or what?' all I can think to say is, 'Yes.' They're all home to me in some special way.

To eight-year-old me, though, Britain was home. I had the clipped English accent to prove it, and a bossy attitude that would set me up for both conflict and success in the United States. My parents were working incredibly hard to get us green cards. It's not an easy process, especially for a pack of artists. At the time, some family friends were visiting from the US, and from them I was learning all kinds of wonderful myths about how flawless America was – and some truths about its natural beauty, history, culture. I was especially excited about learning the swear words. Even so, underneath the allure of a perfect new home, I felt a compulsion that persisted throughout my time there. It was a conditional invitation. 'Welcome,' it said. 'This is your home now. You're American. You speak American.' And so, when we moved, that's what I did, and for the most part I assimilated successfully into our tiny corner of the rural west. Now I had the rounded accent, the cowboy boots and an astonishing tolerance for canned pork and beans.

For the most part, I willingly let go of my ties to home and embraced my new identity. Later, when we were teens, my dad introduced my brother and me to football – proper football. We watched Premier League matches aired on US TV several hours late, meaning we had to studiously ignore the news to avoid results spoilers.

Mostly, though, from the age of nine I watched basketball, and only basketball. I learned American history and only American history. And in all my time in the States there was really only one thing – one consistent thread – that reminded me of my roots. It was music, and specifically some music that became imbued with powerful significance when I was eight years old.

This was about a year before the move, and the precipice we were standing on felt especially real for some reason, like the chasm beyond it spanned the whole Atlantic Ocean.

In my memory, our home in Bath was beautiful in the same way that cancelled TV shows are classic. We left before it could become anything other than perfect.

One day – it must have been late spring or early summer – my dad went away for several weeks. He went to write and record music in his favourite environment – the middle of nowhere, in the Highlands – so my mom, my brother and I went away as well, to the middle of nowhere in rural Devon. We were at some residential event full of grown-ups, and we were pretty much the only kids there.

We could feel the ground shifting beneath us. So we kept to ourselves, to a space we could control. Our imaginary worlds were pretty well developed, thanks to a few years of very limited TV, so we found a bank of earth at the side of a meadow and carved a map into it, a cutaway of rooms hosting characters made of leaves and twigs. We charted stories I can't remember, but they probably involved power struggles between my brother's characters and mine. His creations wore black armour, came from a volcanic mountain range, and their national animal was the bat. They were the morally grey antiheroes to my morally righteous utopians. *We* wore blue and white, *we* lived in cities made of ice, and our national animal was, of course, the ferocious battle unicorn. I was the warrior princess – basically Elsa, before *Frozen* was cool.

My parents were at least partly responsible for this behaviour, always reading poetry, short stories, long stories. In fact, one of my earliest memories is of my mom sitting in a rocking chair – because of course we had a rocking chair – reading me stories when I was very, very small.

In my memory, the rocking chair is enormous, and the stories take up the whole room.

My dad, being a songwriter and incorrigible performer, made up his own stories. They were about a brother and sister called Thundersword and Thundershield – a dynamic duo, an alternate-universe take on my brother and me, where instead of playing in the mud, we fought against an invading force of second-century Roman legions. Thundersword was a fusion of my little brother and a young King Arthur, and Thundershield was inspired by the Celtic chiefess Boudicca, made blonde in my image. Their adventures were fictional and fantastic, starring a band of misfit freedom fighters working to overthrow the very Pythonesque Roman invaders, backed up by a little magic and mysticism. Thundersword and Thundershield always led the charge.

My dad had his own reasons for telling us these stories, and I know the important ones. The first was that he was away a lot, living the life of a modern-day bard, and my mom, in a stroke of genius, saw an opportunity for us to stay in touch via a long, multi-chapter story. We were a little young for *The Lord of the Rings*, so he improvised.

Another reason had to do with identity. My dad has always felt more at home in a tent in the wilderness than in the manicured Surrey suburbs where he grew up, and he wanted us to have a sense of 'home' that was more than just the Queen's England. Rather than stately houses and pathological politeness, Britain to him meant wilderness, deep cultural roots much older than feudalism, a bastion of free thought and rebellious artists. He was in love with the romantic poets and stories of the Celts, of ancient chiefs and torcs and woad war paint and the kind of revolutionary soul that we don't often associate with historical or modern Britain. Finding very little of that spirit in English tradition, he fell in love with the places where it was still a part of their identity – especially Scotland. This was the nineties, which, among other things, was the golden age of Enya and Clannad, and it's why throwback playlists on Spotify never feel quite right to me. My parents loved New Age and world music, and at the time Bath was saturated in both – and our perfect house was saturated in the sounds of Afro-Celt Sound System, Capercaillie and Davy Spillane.

A final reason for my dad's stories was to give both my brother and I an image of human experience that featured strong women and men fighting side by side, to balance out the sexism we were exposed to in wider society. Eventually, years later, he would read *The Lord of the Rings* to us in the months before *The Return of the King* came out in cinemas. And as he read, my dad live-edited the text to make the story less sexist. It took me a reread in my late teens to realise that, canonically speaking, Éowyn sacrifices her independence for Faramir's love. The way I'd heard it, she kept her sword and her status and she got the guy.

Something I didn't understand or appreciate – at least until much, much later – was that my dad's adventures were entirely made up on the fly. This is amazing on a variety of levels, but it unfortunately meant that not only were they not recorded anywhere, but if he wasn't around, there would be no stories. And when I was eight, distracting myself in a muddy bank in Devon, that was exactly what was happening. It was, from my perspective, disastrous timing. We were on the cusp of hearing about a critical battle, our heroes massively outnumbered by the Romans, and suddenly off went my dad to the wilds of Scotland to do his bardic thing. This also wasn't unusual, but the timing was annoying and, as the louder member of his story's two-person fan club, I was appalled at the prospect of waiting for a new chapter.

In retrospect, my jumbled-up emotions about the story were caused by a lot more than a brief mid-season break. Change was in the air. Our move across the Atlantic was on the horizon, and around me were people from all over the world. The Americans were the loudest, and they were telling us all about what our new lives would be like in the new country we would – we must – call home.

And then a package arrived.

In the package was a cassette tape with two sides, loaded with a story made up on the fly and recorded 400 miles north of us. I was excited but also sceptical, because when he's performing, my dad moves constantly, animated by the story he's telling and channelling the characters and the mood all at once. He even does voices. And he did a whole facial-expression thing when performing the Romans, and I really didn't think the comedy would translate without a visual. Surely it wouldn't work without a human being there to give it that *something*, like drama, or a heart, or a soul.

My mom pressed play, and there was my dad's voice – and something else. Music, and definitely not my dad's music or anything else I'd ever heard. It beckoned me in and twirled us across 400 miles of rooftops, mountains, industrial estates, all the way to the wildest places in the British Isles. It threw me into an inter-dimensional gateway almost 2,000 years into the past, laterally across reality to the pocket of improvised world my dad wove with words. I *felt* so strongly; I connected to the words and sank into the story in a way I'd never done before. I cascaded through emotions, from the euphoric opening track to the death scene. And yes, there was a death scene. And I think if my dad had known how much that scene would make me cry, thanks to the heartbreakingly sad soundtrack, he would never have included it.

As with most things from that year, the story is hazy but the feelings are crystal clear. I don't remember most details of *my own* story that year either, but I do remember feelings and snapshots. It's possible that had that tape not arrived, the summer would have been swallowed up by the chaos of pre-immigration anxiety and I wouldn't have remembered today that there were stories at all. One of my least-favourite idioms is 'Hindsight is 20/20,' because I don't really remember most of my eight-year-old self. I can't even do the accent properly any more. Hindsight gets blurrier the further back I go and, far enough down the line, reality seems even more tenuous than it did when I was eight. But after the move, when I was old enough to discover my own tastes in music, I came back to this album and I *felt* everything. I still do.

My dad's stories gave me all kinds of complexes. I love military history, Celtic imagery and music, I have a thing for strong, independent women.

More than anything, though, I'm in love with stories, with the fact that every time we experience one, a whole new universe exists, even for the briefest moment. Our reality and the storyteller's collide, and feelings ensue, and if that's not the closest we can get to visiting another dimension, I don't know what is. Music has these unbelievable powers over our hearts and minds, and it can make those dimensions vibrant in indescribable ways.

For a long time I wanted to make music for a living, and I thought that my dad's tapes had taught me about the importance of soundtracks, but they were more than that. I make stories for a living now and I realise that they taught me about storytelling, in all its forms. They taught me to recognise those parallel worlds and to appreciate how fleeting they can be. And they taught me a secret: if you have the right key, those brief universes are places you can go back to.

The stories my dad told were a miniature of home, a snowglobe, an anchor for a kid on the precipice of a new home and a new identity. The song that changed my life is my key to that place. It's by a Scottish musician called Dougie MacLean, and before you listen to it, I want to invite you into that tiny universe. Put yourself at just over four feet tall, eight years old, watching the wheels in a cassette like they're the eyes of a storyteller...

'Perthshire Amber'
Written by Dougie MacLean
Performed by Dougie MacLean
Taken from the album *Perthshire Amber*, released in 1999

Apple Music   Spotify

This story was first performed as part of *OneTrackMinds* Hidden Tracks at Omeara London on 24 July 2018.

Rosa Dachtler is a writer for video games with a deep love of fantasy and history. She grew up in Europe and the US and still can't decide which feels more like home.

Inua Ellams

This is not really a boy-meets-girl story. It's more a boy-who-never-met-a-girl story.

I was born in Nigeria in 1984, into a very matriarchal household, and I have three sisters: an older sister, a twin sister and a little sister. They were my everything. We were equals. In Nigerian culture it's suggested that the twin who comes out second is the older twin because she sends the other one out of the womb to check out the world, make sure it is OK. So my twin sister has always sort of been like the boss of me. She bullied me, and I tried to bully her back. I failed all the time.

And I had an older sister who was this figure of authority, and a little sister who I cared for. So I was surrounded by very strong powerful women. And because of that, I had no interest in other girls, as such.

We left Nigeria in 1996. I came to London, and I went to Holland Park School, and there were all sorts of ready distractions to keep me away from the sphere of heteronormative romance. Specifically, there was basketball, which I played a lot of. There was athletics, and I discovered hip-hop, which I didn't really like when I was in Nigeria. But I began to spend most of my time in the art rooms, drawing. I was fascinated by visual arts and I wanted to be a painter.

In my first couple of weeks in London, my best friend – a guy called Jack – introduced me to his best friend – a girl called Golnar. She'd sit across from me in the art room and just give me really bad, evil looks, and I was too nervous to say anything. I thought, *Why? We haven't swapped a word! Where's all this bile and venom coming from?*

She just stared at me.

I remember it was around Christmas, and I had to give everyone Christmas cards, as you do when you're a twelve-year-old. I wrote a card saying, 'If you want to talk to me, then just come on and do so. Don't give me dirty looks.'

And that was the first time we communicated. I began to develop a crush on her. I was twelve years old, and that was my first ever crush. But she was not interested. Twelve-year-old girls tend to be interested in older boys, those in the years above who grab their attention. I was just nothing to her.

She would come to watch the guys play basketball – I think that's why I started playing properly – but she wasn't watching me. She was watching those older guys with six-packs, who could jump and dunk. I was just this scrawny little Nigerian rat.

I had this crush on her for about three years. When I finally plucked up the courage to tell her, it was in the playground. I was fifteen years old and there was no one else around.

I told her that I had told one of her best friends that she was the nicest girl in school. And she told me that she had just told one of her friends that she thought I was one of the nicest boys in school.

I remember thinking, 'We've had three years! You could have done this anytime! And nothing…'

But that summer my family ran into difficulties, and we had to leave London and move to Dublin. Just when I thought we'd cracked the ice, I had to move to Ireland! This was 1999, and when we arrived there, I discovered I was the only Black boy in the entire school. Dublin in the early nineties was quite a difficult place to be if you were an African kid. There was a lot of racism, ignorance, a lot of stereotypes around for Black boys, which I could have comfortably slid in to to be accepted. They believed Black boys all played basketball and were good at it. Fine, I liked that stereotype. I played – but I wasn't really good. Another stereotype was that I would have a sort of encyclopaedic knowledge of hip-hop music and culture. This I severely lacked. They also thought I'd be really good, naturally gifted at athletics, which I wasn't – I was just OK. All I really wanted to do was spend time painting in the art rooms.

I also discovered that it wasn't really cool to hang out with the Black kid. It was a taboo to be my friend – let alone to be my girlfriend. The idea of any kind of romance belonged this other world that I was not privy to. It never seemed achievable. While my basketball team-mates, raging with hormones, had girlfriends to help them figure out how to manage those emotions, it was a world I couldn't explore. I was shut out of it because I was Black.

I'd walk through shopping malls, for instance, and people would squirt mustard on me. I'd be cycling home and people would shoulder-charge me off my bicycle and onto the pavement. I'd be playing basketball and the whole auditorium would be screaming racially offensive insults, chanting the N-word and its various incarnations.

As you can imagine, it made life really, really difficult.

And it made the idea of attracting or approaching women feel completely impossible. I felt incredibly unwanted and unattractive. I returned to London in 2001 to visit Jack, and I remember we went to his house in Westbourne Park. We listened to music, and he played me an album by a musician called Musiq Soulchild. Quite a name, I thought... The soul child of music.

It was part of a new genre called neo soul, and I loved it. There was a song called '143', which I still think to this day is one of the most beautiful songs about love that I've ever heard. But there was one particular song called 'Just Friends', which I asked him to play over and over again. Rather than the braggadocio of hip-hop and gangsta rap, which seemed to dominate the Black musical landscape in Dublin, this was a man singing beautifully and politely about romance, about asking someone out.

I had never heard anything like it, and the lyrics captured all the things I was too nervous to say because of who I was and how I was perceived in Dublin. I had never felt as though I could approach girls, but this song captured all the ways I would if I could.

So I did the one thing I could that made sense to me. When I got back to Dublin, I copied the song onto a tape, and I carried it around with me everywhere, hoping that I'd find a girl who I was brave enough to give it to. Because I couldn't speak to her, this tape would do all the heavy lifting for me. It was in my back pocket everywhere I went. I carried it to basketball courts, I carried it to lessons; through shopping malls and city centres, it was there.

I carried it for eighteen months in total, and I never gave it to anyone.

I still have that tape.

It is under my bed right now in Brixton. And I think what I realised from this experience was the precision of culture and of language. In certain ways it's one of the reasons I began to write, because I realised that there are whole worlds and nuances and ways of being in that song, which spoke for me. And I wanted to be able to do that, to attend to that sort of alchemy, for myself, and for others who could not speak.

'Just Friends (Sunny)'
Written by Carvin Haggins, Bobby Hebb and Taalib Johnson
Performed by Musiq Soulchild
Taken from the album *Aijuswanaseing*, released on Def Soul in 2000

Apple Music   Spotify

This story was first performed at Wilton's Music Hall on 1 June 2018.

Inua Ellams is an internationally touring poet, playwright, performer, graphic artist and designer. He is an ambassador for the Ministry of Stories and his published books of poetry include *Candy Coated Unicorns and Converse All Stars*, *Thirteen Fairy Negro Tales*, *The Wire-Headed Heathen*, *Afterhours* and *The Half-God of Rainfall* – an epic story in verse. His first play, *The 14th Tale*, was awarded a Fringe First at the Edinburgh International Theatre Festival and his fourth, *Barber Shop Chronicles*, sold out two runs at England's National Theatre. He is currently touring *An Evening with an Immigrant* and recently published his first full poetry collection, *The Actual*. In graphic art and design, online and in print he tries to mix the old with the new, juxtaposing texture and pigment with flat shades of colour and vector images. He lives and works from London, where he founded the Midnight Run, a nocturnal urban excursion. He is a Fellow of the Royal Society of Literature.

Janice Johnson

The song I've chosen has been in my head for as long as I can remember. The trouble is, 'as long as I can remember' doesn't quite stretch back as far as most people would assume. My memory has always been stubbornly incomplete. Most of my younger years are nothing but barely visible shadows in the darkest depths of my mind. So, 'Gimme Hope Jo'anna' is more of a soundtrack, one that changes my life a little every time I hear it, and always for the better.

'Gimme Hope Jo'anna' doesn't bring back the missing pages or chapters from my life's story. I don't think anything ever could. Somehow, though, it almost immediately fills in the gaps – floods them, even – in a different way. It colours them in, not with words or pictures, but with a visceral rush of pure joy and warmth that feels undeniable, like a concrete connection to those missing moments I can only access this way. So really, when I look back, I feel as though this song actually came into my life before I even knew I was here.

No one else in my immediate family seems to have this memory problem. Between them, my mother, father, brothers and sister remember practically all of the decade that I've lost. I've always found that fascinating. My dad will tell you that he even has memories of experiences he had as far back as when he was three years old, something which I've never quite been able to get my head around. He has an almost photographic memory, which is pretty impressive. It's not just the important things, either; he remembers the most bizarre, random facts about things no reasonable brain has any business remembering. It's all up there, waiting for the right moment to strike.

Sometimes I wish I were able to look back like that and see a whole album of snapshots from every year of my life. The fact remains, though, that I don't have an album of memories that I can trace back that far. When I look in my mind's eye, it's like being in a huge house with great big frames lining the walls. Sometimes a quick flicker of something will flash inside one of them. It looks like it might become a fully developed picture, but just as it starts to take form, it disappears again. So, every frame is empty, waiting for the pictures that might fill it one day – all except three. I don't know why or how these three pictures made it on to these walls. For whatever reason, though, there they are – shadowy, but there.

A fork... A shadow on a wall... Piano fingers... It probably doesn't seem like a priceless collection, but there is at least some meaning in the mess.

A fork

I've often wondered why I remember the fork. I haven't found an answer to that question yet. It happened in the blink of an eye – well, it must have, because in this flash of a memory there's no before or after, just a fork heading towards me in slow motion and hyperspeed all at the same time.

Life in a big family is full of these split-second moments, and my family is *very* big. Living in Ghana, my siblings and I were surrounded by aunties and uncles, grandmothers and grandfathers and everything in between. Then there were the cousins, a little band of mischief-makers. For the adults, looking after us all meant they had to have eyes in the back of their head.

The fork came towards me. A second later I felt a searing pain shoot through my arm. The fork's pointy tines had landed square in my armpit, leaving four perfectly even holes behind. It turned out that on the other end of this fork was my little cousin Anthony. He was just old enough to know that he shouldn't have done it, but young enough to be forgiven for it – after he'd been well and truly reprimanded by my auntie, of course.

Then there's nothing more; the memory bank closes and we're back to the void. No aftermath, no healing, nothing but the scar I was left with, which faded over the years... until it just disappeared, as everything does eventually. Maybe that's what keeps the fork in my mind. Maybe it's a reminder that we never really know what's around the corner. Maybe it's a reminder that in a split second life can change in a way that we can't see coming because, as much as we'd like to, we don't have eyes in the backs of our heads. Maybe it's a call to remember that painful things happen, but at some point the pain will end, the scars will fade to nothing and a new day will begin again.

A shadow on the wall

In 1990 my family and I left the UK and moved to Ghana. We stayed with my auntie Mary and several other family members. Her house – just one part of a large compound – was whitewashed right up to the roof. In the evenings the outdoor lights cast long, dark shadows on the walls. I remember once standing by one of those walls and watching my shadow dance across it as I laughed uncontrollably. I'm not sure why I was laughing or who I was laughing with.

It wasn't just me and my shadow; there was someone else there, another child, but I'm not sure who. It could have been one of my cousins, or maybe a sibling. I can't quite make them out in the picture in my mind. What I do see, though, is my head swinging back again and again as I laughed. The more I laughed the more my sides hurt, and the more they hurt the more I held on to them, until I was crouched down, half laughing, half crying, on the floor.

My family will tell you that I've always been that way. My mum even delights in predicting it. 'Oh wait,' she'll say in Ga. 'Just wait, she'll laugh so hard she'll be crying any second now.' And I always do, right on cue. I just can't help it, and anyway, if laughter really is the best medicine, then I'm not about to stop now. I'm still never too far from tears when I laugh. When I see that picture in my mind, I know exactly how it felt to laugh and cry in that moment. It felt good. It felt joyous, innocent and good.

It felt like freedom.

Piano fingers

We said goodbye to the freedom of Accra in 1991 and returned to an uncertain future in London. Our family's fortunes had taken an unexpected turn, so for a time there was less laughter, but we always found joy where we could. When Eddy Grant was playing, there was *always* joy.

I started at a new primary school with my brothers and sister. It was the first time the five of us had all gone to the same school at the same time, which makes me smile. I can just imagine a group of little button-nosed kids on their way to school, holding hands in height order, with the tallest leading the way. In reality, I don't think it was anything like that. My mum was probably trying to keep us all together and in one piece on the short journey from our house to the school, which stood at the end of the same road. My made-up image still makes me smile, though.

My little brothers spent their days in the school nursery. My parents say that every day my school friend and I would walk across the playground to peer through the wire fence that separated the nursery from the school playground, just to make sure that they were all right. While we checked on the twins, the dinner ladies checked on us. I remember a moment with a couple of them. They were standing by a lamp pole in the centre of the playground with their arms folded across their chests. They were like a power-posing dinner-lady tag team, ready to swoop in and save the day with plasters and a first-aid kit the second anyone's knee hit the ground.

My friend and I had gone to ask them a question. I don't remember what it was, but I know I demonstrated some action with my hands as I said it. The dinner lady commented on my hands and asked if I played the piano. When I told her I didn't, she insisted that I went to see the music teacher straight away and start having lessons. According to her, I had 'lovely long piano fingers', which not everyone had, so I should give it some serious thought. I remember looking at my hands and wondering how many lessons I would need to have to become an expert.

Years later, that dinner lady's words form one of the only pictures hanging in the frames in my mind. I never had piano lessons, but I've been asked the same question by more people than I can remember. I guess she was right: I do have piano fingers. Maybe one day, I'll finally learn to play properly. I did teach myself to play 'My Heart Will Go On' from *Titanic*, and I can play a mean rendition of 'London's Burning' on the recorder too. It's not exactly Mozart, but it's good enough for me.

Individually, these memories don't make much meaningful sense of anything, but hearing 'Gimme Hope Jo'anna' instantly seems to connect them all perfectly in my mind, without the need for any explanation – it just is what it is. When I think about my story, there are lots of moments that could be more detailed – more fleshed out and whole – that are unhelpfully blurry and meagre instead. I wonder what it was like to to live in those moments. I might never know for sure, but I can feel it. Every time I hear this song I know that no matter what life was like or what I did and didn't have, there were times when I danced, I laughed and I was happy.

Of course, I know life during my early years wasn't pain-free. I know it wasn't all rainbows and unicorns, and neither is this song. As happy and upbeat as it sounds, 'Gimme Hope Jo'anna' is a protest song. The lyrics are a hard-hitting rage against the apartheid regime in South Africa. Grant sings about a racist ruling class that murdered and brutalised its citizens. It's about the misery of living in constant fear of murder; it's about police brutality and mistreatment of innocent people; and it's about the oppressive injustice Black South Africans were subjected to while they endured the cruelty of poverty, corruption and the destruction of their nation. It's the definition of a bitter-sweet song – a tune that I love paired with words that I wish had never needed to be written.

What hits me when I hear it, though, is more than just the lyrics. I hear a colourful, iridescent sound that fills the empty frames hanging in my mind. It's almost impossible not to be moved by that. I hear the hope of freedom in the song and the joy of complete inhibition in how my body responds to it. More than anything, it just makes me *feel*. I'm told that I knew all the lyrics by heart as a child, but I doubt I knew what they meant back then; I probably just liked that it was a loud, high-energy song with a beat that made me want to dance and a melody that made me want to sing.

Looking back, though, I can see many ways in which the song resonates with me. What stands out the most is that it's a song about a beautiful country, where people lived peacefully as part of a community that was shattered by circumstances out of their control. It tells the story of finding meaning in circumstances we might not have wished for, but have to go through anyway.

'Gimme Hope Jo'anna' is, of course, ultimately a song of hope. Woven into every one of the terrible circumstances in the story Grant tells is hope for a better future. His words acknowledge that life isn't perfect, that we never know what's around the corner. His words make it clear that sometimes, even if everything from the places you call home to the people you love are taken away from you, your pain really can fade to nothing. You can find joy in the shadows, and whether you're sitting at the piano or listening through a speaker, you can choose to play a soundtrack to your life that gives you hope for the future.

'Gimme Hope Jo'anna'
Written by Eddy Grant
Performed by Eddy Grant
Taken from the album *File Under Rock*, released on Parlophone in
1988

Apple Music   Spotify

This story was first performed at the House of St Barnabas on
16 May 2019.

Janice Johnson is founder of Eating With Elephants, which tackles
loneliness and social isolation through coaching, workshops and
storytelling dinners, where strangers gather to share stories about
their elephant in the room. She lives in London and is a fan of
campfires, lunch and dinner tables, looking up from screens and
other things that lead to powerful conversations and good old
authentic human connection.

Richard McDougall

Sometimes I get a quiet thrill if I see a celebrity or somebody in authority making a bit of a chump of themselves in public. But I have to confess to a pang of empathy for the Tory politician John Redwood, who, some years ago, while serving as the Minister for Wales, was caught by the BBC pretending to sing along to the Welsh national anthem. He was caught on camera just at the moment when everyone was standing up to sing. And, just at that moment, John Redwood must have realised that he didn't know the words. Thinking on his feet, he decided to move his head from side to side and open and close his mouth creatively in the hope that these combined movements would be enough to create an illusion that would fool all of those watching.

Well, you didn't need to be a professional magician to know he wasn't fooling anybody. And by the look of terror in his eyes, he knew that we knew that he knew that he wasn't fooling anybody...

I'm telling you this because not only do I not know the words to the Welsh national anthem, I struggle to remember the words to any songs whatsoever. I love music – I listen to music every single day, and I've heard some songs hundreds, maybe thousands of times – but for some reason the words just don't seem to go in. I've had many John Redwood moments. Even a classic like 'Hey Jude' by the Beatles stumps me. After I've sung the first two words, I'm not really on terra firma until we get to the 'na-na-ba' bits at the end. I think it's something to do with getting caught up in the rhythm of it, because it's a problem that's not just confined to music. I had been doing yoga classes for many years, until one day we had a change of teacher. The new teacher finished in exactly the same way as the old yoga teacher always finished, by putting his hands together and saying, 'Namaste.' Everybody else in the class put their hands together and said, 'Namaste.' And I was dumbfounded. Because for all that time I'd thought we'd been saying 'Have a nice day'...

But there is one song whose words are branded onto my heart. And I know exactly where I was when I first heard it. I must have been about seven years old at the time, and my father was standing next to me. When the singing started, he turned to me and he had tears in his bright blue eyes. Now, I knew he wasn't sad, because he was smiling. But at seven I didn't quite understand the dynamics of the emotion on his face. All I knew was that it was the song that had triggered the tears.

We were in a church at the time. Well, I say a church... It's not a church in the conventional sense of the term, but it's a place of communal togetherness, spiritual endeavours. I think a church is a very good word. We were at Anfield, the home of Liverpool Football Club. And the song that started my father's tears was 'You'll Never Walk Alone.'

Now, I know there'll be some people reading this who are really not interested in football. And I know there'll be some people reading this who *are* interested in football, but really *not* interested in Liverpool Football Club. But if we could just step outside of our respective Venn diagrams for a moment and leave apathy and tribalism to one side, I'd like to share with you why this one song has been like a piece of Kevlar thread that's been there throughout my life, and the impact it still has on me today.

I was born and raised in Liverpool, and, along with my brother and sister, was brought up as a Liverpool supporter, like my father and, indeed, like his father before him. In fact, it was my grandfather's seats that we were using that day at Anfield, and I still remember holding my father's hand and walking through the streets of Liverpool on our way to the match, where first it was a trickle and then a stream, and then a river of red, all moving in the same direction. I can remember walking through the clanking, claustrophobic turnstiles, up a set of stone steps, along a corridor, up some more stone steps and through a little gap, where my face was splashed by the luminescence of the green that was underneath my feet.

In those days fans used to stand on the terraces, so away to my right there were 26,000 people crammed into the Kop, already in full voice, waiting for their heroes to emerge. And when they did, and they started to sing 'You'll Never Walk Alone', as they always do, those first opening mournful lines swirled around the ground, reaching a thunderous climax that crashed against the inside of my head and washed through me.

It's a wonderful song, and wherever you sing it, it's pretty special. But when you're singing as part of a choir of 50,000 voices, it's simply unforgettable.

In the 1970s we moved down south to London, so visits to Anfield were few and far between, and we had to make do with listening to the games on *Sports Report* on BBC Radio 2. Best of all were the European nights, the midweek games, when we'd start in the kitchen, all huddled around the Roberts radio. And even there the ferocity and intensity of 'You'll Never Walk Alone' seemed to burst through the radio. And even there there would be tears in my father's blue eyes. And then we'd all have to go upstairs and do our homework, try and concentrate on our geography, our rivers and our mountains. But our ears were on full alert to see if there was any disturbance from downstairs. And every now and then the silence would be punctuated by a sharp clapping sound and a mad shuffling of feet in the kitchen, and the lounge doors being flung open as my both my parents burst out, trying to be the first to the bottom of the stairs (usually it was my father), just so they could be the one that would shout out, 'Keegan, one–nil!' And we'd scramble down as fast as we could, we'd be jumping up and down, and my dad would be trying to shush us; he probably had tears in his eyes, but he wanted to hear the replay. And more often than not during that glorious time, it was just three simple words – 'Heighway, Toshack, Keegan' – and then we'd go back upstairs and do our homework again, and come back down towards the end of the game to hear the final whistle. And always, always, one more chorus of 'You'll Never Walk Alone'.

Now, every club wants to have a great song. Fans have spent hours in pubs and bars, cars and coaches and trains on the way to matches, trying to write the words that will ignite their team and push them forward. But for some reason Liverpool took a song from a Hollywood musical, the theatre show *Carousel*, with music and lyrics by Rodgers and Hammerstein. It was back in the 1960s when they first started singing it. I've often wondered how it happened... I picture a bunch of Scousers sitting in a pub with a pen and paper, sitting in silence, trying to find other words that rhyme with Liverpool. And then the door bursts open, and another scouser comes in and says, 'Put your pens down, lads – I've got the perfect song. And you're not gonna believe *where* I found it...'

(*Carousel* is a great show, by the way.)

The song fitted Liverpool. In the mid- to late twentieth century so many British cities suffered from social urban decline, high

111

unemployment and their own specific tragedies. And Liverpool was no exception. Those words – 'you'll never walk alone' – seemed to fit not only the relationship between the team and the fans, but the relationship between the people of Liverpool and the very city itself.

When I was eighteen, I came home from school one day and was told that my father had died suddenly from a heart attack. He was fifty-one. I didn't go to football matches any more, but my brother and sister did – they'd mercifully kept hold of the season tickets. And they'd hold up the phone, and I could still hear the words loud and clear, even though I was 200 miles away.

And now I have two boys of my own. And when they were the right age, I was lucky enough to take each of them in turn and hold their hand and walk through those same streets that I walked through with my father, following that red line to the ground. We walked through those same claustrophobic clanking turnstiles, up that same set of stairs, across that corridor, up that final set of stairs and through that little gap, where they too were baptised in the green water beneath. And when the crowd started to sing 'You'll Never Walk Alone', and that red wall rose away to my right, I turned to look at each of my boys, and they saw tears in my eyes. To this day, I'm not really sure why my father was crying – passion, pride, heritage, belonging. I certainly feel all of these. But more than that, it's because just for a few moments my dad is standing next to me again, with a smile on his face and tears in his bright blue eyes...

'You'll Never Walk Alone'
Written by Richard Rodgers and Oscar Hammerstein
Performed by Gerry and the Pacemakers and the Anfield Kop,
April 2016

YouTube

This story was first performed at Wilton's Music Hall on 1 June 2018.

Richard McDougall is a magician, public speaker and business coach. He is a gold-star member of the Magic Circle, and is a World Open champion in close-up magic. He has co-written TV shows for Derren Brown and appeared on BBC, Channel 4 and ITV. Nowadays much of his time is dedicated to working with Breathe Arts Health Research, adapting magic tricks to use as therapy for those living with disabilities.

Nicholas Jessup

I am an over-apologiser. A sorry-sayer. I know the full range of its uses – and abuses. I can say all manner of sorrys in a single day, from the one where I hold the door open for someone else, to the one I say too soon in an argument.

To understand my 'sorry' syndrome, it's helpful to understand my family background. My parents separated when I was still quite young, and it is a long acknowledged fact within my family that, as the youngest child, I am the physical embodiment of my father's last apology to my mother. So maybe apologies are just encoded into my DNA.

When I was seven years old, my mum, my brother Chris and I were on the trip of a lifetime, driving around New Zealand visiting my mum's side of the family. At one of my aunties' houses, my brother and I were playing on the front lawn when suddenly, from nowhere, a huge Alsatian came barrelling towards us.

It was enormous. And it was angry. It showed no sign of stopping.

We fled back towards the house. Chris, being older and bigger than me, got there first. So, naturally, he slammed the door in my face to celebrate, leaving me at the mercy of this beast.

When I finally recovered consciousness, he didn't apologise. Nor did I expect him to. Older brothers never do. On the other hand, he did teach me all I needed to know about Darwinism and imbued in me a competitive spirit that has seen my family abandon all manner of Christmas board games.

Thanks to having three older siblings, I was ahead of the curve compared to my school friends when it came to all things cultural. Thanks to my brothers' and sister's viewing habits, I was au fait with with *Dawson's Creek*, *Blossom*, *Friends* and *The OC* way before any of my contemporaries. The same with film as well – we watched *The Goonies*, *Dick Tracy* and *Terminator 2: Judgment Day* – all films that have directly led to my passion for and desire to work in the film industry. My brothers also showed me the film *Arachnophobia*, which directly led to my arachnophobia.

And, of course, there was music. There is a direct causal link between my sister's teenage love of Take That and my unadulterated infatuation with NSync.

But it was my oldest brother Olly who had the biggest cultural impact on me when he introduced me to the song that changed my life during Christmas of 1996.

My dad had recently moved to the US, and we were facing up to Christmas without him. Nineteen ninety-six was a year in which music had already begun to worm its way into my life.

I was nine and getting to an age where I understood that I could have my own taste. Nursery rhymes had lost their sheen. I was jaded, secretly hoping for a packet of Marlboro Reds at the bottom of my stocking. My mum was trying with all of her might and will to make this Christmas 'normal', and there was lots of excitement about Olly coming home from university.

To paint an image of where he was in his life, he was sporting a shaved head – full cue-ball bald – a red-and-black lumberjack shirt with a hat to match and a general overarching broodiness. He was entering his grunge stage. His hi-fi blasted out Seattle-based shredders like Nirvana and Pearl Jam. He smelled of an intoxicating mixture of incense and cigarettes. I was never quite sure which one was meant to mask the smell of the other.

Suddenly, traditions took hold. New traditions. Stockings to be opened at dawn, presents with nibbles at eleven – and then lunch in all of its apologetic loveliness at three.

One tradition, which has been carried over to this day, and stems from the fact that I was once the smallest member of the family, is that I got the job of handing out the presents from under the tree.

We were getting down to the last few gifts – and by that I mean the smallest ones. As yet no one had opened a gift from Olly, and he was unusually quiet. We were used to him grunting, but not silence.

I reached under the tree and grabbed a densely packed small box.

I inspected the tag; it simply said 'I'm sorry'. Olly quickly grunted that this gift was for all of us.

One box, for all of us.

But who would unwrap it?

Well, I would, obviously. I was the youngest, after all, and therefore the one with the strongest claim to be the centre of attention.

When I unpacked the gift, it was a collection of cassette singles, some of which still bore the 99p price tag from the local record store in Burgess Hill.

My brother, it turns out, had invested most of his student loan in beer. And now he was broke. These tapes were all he could afford.

He was so utterly embarrassed.

We didn't even know whose tape was whose.

116

Again I got to choose first, and I naturally gravitated towards the one tape that had every rebellious young boy's musical seal of approval emblazoned on its cover – PARENTAL ADVISORY EXPLICIT LYRICS. That black-and-white logo contained the four sweetest words in the English language for me and was a gateway to learning some even sweeter words to expel on the playground when school came back round. To a kid that had already seen *Terminator 2*, these words were sacred.

The song was by Tupac Shakur, and when I first listened to it, I was immediately hooked. I needed to know everything about him. I pressed my brother for as much information as I could. No sooner had I found my new idol than I found out that he was in fact dead. The song my brother had bought me was his first posthumous release.

Tupac's music had such a profound effect on me that I wrote about him for a creative-writing element of my English Literature GCSE coursework. I quoted him in my A-level exam about Shakespeare's *Othello*. Later on, I tattooed his record-company logo on my arm (this was around the same time I had dreadlocks). While at university, I founded a business and named it Concrete Rose after some of his poems. Tupac was everything to me, and he shaped my life in ways my brother could not have known when he was in that record store in Burgess Hill.

He definitely did not need to apologise for that.

This is what siblings do. Especially if you are lucky enough to have older ones. They leave indelible marks all over you. Marks I now wear as a badge of honour.

My family is not normal. Thankfully. But they are my family, and I do need to tell them all I am sorry – because I should tell them I love them more often.

'I Ain't Mad at Cha'
Written by Tupac Shakur and Danny Steward
Performed by 2Pac featuring Danny Boy
Taken from the album *All Eyez on Me*, released on
Death Row Records in 1996

Apple Music

Spotify

This story was first performed as part of *OneTrackMinds* Hidden Tracks at Omeara London on 24 July 2018.

Nicholas Jessup is a screenwriter and sometime producer based in London, by way of Brighton, Los Angeles, Te'Awamutu and Wilmington, Delaware. Nick (to his friends) suffers from malusdomesticaphobia – an irrational fear of apples. Despite this, he has worked in the TV and film industry for the better part of a decade, ranging from live broadcast to feature film, documentary and music videos.

Alice Martin

I would like to share with you a story about my mother, and a song she shared with me. This song has been an anchor, a port in a storm, for me on several occasions.

But first, let me start by telling you about Ma.

My mother was born in Glasgow in 1940. She was the eldest of five children. As the eldest, it was up to her to keep the younger ones entertained playing outside. These games were often inspired by their weekly trips to the pictures on Saturday mornings to watch the Hollywood musicals. They would return home to re-enact those tales, and they were so in love with the glamour, the gowns, the music, the dancing. She was proud of the fact that they could make their own fun.

Keeping the younger ones entertained outside in Scotland's inclement weather was sometimes tough, but when the little ones started to tire and whine, Ma would distract them with a story or a song.

Ma was very bright. She taught herself to read aged four, and waited for the right moment to showcase this new skill. One morning at home she asked her parents for some new story books, which were in short supply at that time. Paying little attention, her parents told her that books were for children who could read. Even now I can imagine the pleasure in her defiant little face as she picked up her father's newspaper and, measuring out the words in the front-page headline with one chubby finger, read aloud, 'Mur-Der In Soho'. After that, she was allowed free access to the family's *Encyclopaedia Britannica*.

After studying at Glasgow university, Ma moved to London to work as a teacher. Twenty or so years later, I was born. And now her ability to distract with stories came into its own, because we used to walk everywhere, and there is nothing more useful to keep a discontented child on side than with a story – preferably one in which that child has a starring role.

She would tell me a story – often about 'how Alice saves the day' – and distract me from my tired legs. When she paused, I would nag at her, asking, 'Now what, Mummy, now what?' and my reluctant steps quickened with the pace of the tale as the story would miraculously reach a triumphant conclusion just as we reached our destination.

Despite my desire to be the hero of her tales, this story is about how *Ma* saved the day – as she did in the summer I turned eight, when she realised I couldn't read. At all. I was at a very progressive school in Brent, and they believed you would learn to read when you were ready. But there's a difference between being willing and being able. Ma started by asking me why I had such an aversion to print. Rather than admit I had no idea how to make sense of all the hostile-looking squiggles, I told her that I thought the Peter and Jane books we were forced to read were boring and sexist.

And they were.

Until Ma rewrote them for me. When the new stories were about how *Daddy* and Peter bake a cake. While *Mummy* and Jane steal a car...

In 2006, during a gap year, I moved to China to teach English. When I arrived, I realised that the teacher training that the gap-year company had organised was a lot less comprehensive than I had expected. I was introduced to a room of over thirty students. The introduction was a very one-way process – the headmaster told me that I wouldn't be able to remember all their names, but that it didn't matter, as each child was given a number. I was expected to ask questions and call out a number, and the child assigned to that number would answer.

I was aghast because this was nothing like anything I'd ever experienced. I felt adrift. So I called Ma for her advice.

And she told me to teach them with songs.

So that's what I did. I stood in front of every class I had, and I sang a 'happy refrain' to them – out of tune and unashamed. They laughed at me, but that was OK because I saw that we connected.

In 2013 I married my wonderful husband Daniel, and I gave birth to twin girls. Ma was so excited. She promised me that when I went back to work, she'd look after the babies, saving us a fortune in childcare costs. She said it'd be easy for her, as she only lived about twenty minutes away.

It was a wonderful idea, but somehow I knew that it wouldn't be possible. I had started to notice a quite alarming absent-mindedness in her.

When I was still on maternity leave, Ma would pop over most days. She'd call to tell me that she was on her way. But sometimes twenty minutes would go by and she still hadn't arrived. And then thirty minutes…

I'd open the door and look outside and find her in our street, just walking up and down, unable to remember which house was mine.

On Pancake Day it really hit me. Ma came over with a recipe book (which must have been as old as I was) and the ingredients for making pancakes. In my kitchen I watched as she opened the book and scanned the pages, but as her attention flicked between the words and the ingredients, I saw confusion cloud her face. Somehow, it didn't compute. She couldn't see how these items and these words connected. It was like the foundation of her understanding had become unreliable. It was no longer holding fast. To try and keep things bright and breezy, I stepped in to make the pancakes while she sang to the babies.

Not long after this, Ma was diagnosed with Alzheimer's. It's a progressive disease, a degenerative one, and the confusion rapidly got worse.

In 2016 I moved to Zurich in Switzerland for work. It was an amazing opportunity and wonderful for our family, but I missed my parents, and I was concerned about not being there to see how Ma's illness was progressing. My dad stopped work so he could care for her (really, he's the hero of this story). As such, they were able to come over to Switzerland to visit us quite often – which was wonderful.

For my dad's birthday in 2017 they came over to see us to celebrate. I wanted to arrange a special trip to mark his birthday but also to acknowlege how amazingly well he was caring for Ma. They flew out to Zurich, and then the six of us – Ma and Dad, the twins, my husband and I – drove for three hours through the beautiful mountains to Lake Como.

Two things became very clear very quickly. Firstly, Lake Como is one of the most beautiful places on earth. Secondly, I had grossly underestimated the strain that this trip was going to put on Ma. She was afraid. She was anxious. She was completely and utterly lost. She didn't understand what was going on or where we were. And she was not afraid to let us know how she felt.

When we got home to Zurich, I was relieved. It had been an exhausting trip. But there was no relief for Ma. I found her walking around downstairs, opening doors, looking in bags. She came to me to tell me that something terrible had happened. She told me that she'd lost her daughter. Her daughter Alice.

I told her no, that wasn't true, I was right here.

And she looked at me, utterly bewildered by this explanation.

'No, dear,' she told me. 'You are a grown-up woman. Alice – my Alice – is just a little girl.'

I took her hand and told her I understood. I told her, 'It's OK. Little Alice is with me. I'm looking after her for you. But she asked me to give you a message. She wants you to know that she's fine. She's safe. She's happy. And she loves you. And she misses you.'

And that seemed to sink in, because Ma did settle and calm down. She slept pretty well that night.

So now what, Ma? Now what?

Ma's not really up to trips abroad these days. So I see her every time I'm back in the country. And I love that. In the interim we have a lot of video calls. Sometimes Ma is really perky. She likes to do introductions – 'Hello, my name is Maggie, and this is my husband Andy.'

I say, 'Hi, Ma, hi, Dad.'

Puzzled, she asks, 'Why do you call me Ma?'

I reply, 'Because you're my mother.'

And she says – gently, kindly, because she really doesn't want to hurt my feelings – 'It's nice that you think of me that way.'

One of the results of Ma's Alzheimer's (and I say Ma's Alzheimer's, because it is different for everyone) is that she doesn't like to wash.

So when I visit, I try to engage her, soothe her and cajole her into the shower with me. I tell her it'll be a mother-daughter spa day.

I put on some music, and I sing to her – out of tune and unashamed. And it's OK, because we connect.

She doesn't always recognise me.

But she recognises love.

This is the song I sing to her. It's the song I know inspired her as a girl. It's the song I sang in front of hundreds of students in China, and it's the song I sing to reconnect with my mother even when she doesn't know me.

It's my happy refrain, because although we are living daily with the grief and the loss, as long as there is an anchor of love, then despite the pain, we are singing, and dancing, in the rain...

'Singin' in the Rain'
Written by Arthur Freed and Nacio Herb Brown
Performed by Gene Kelly
Taken from the soundtrack to the film *Singin' in the Rain*,
released on MGM Records in 1952

Apple Music   Spotify

This story was first performed at *OneTrackMinds* Hidden Tracks at Omeara London on 14 January 2018.

Alice Martin is an international private-client lawyer. She advises clients in the arts, media and digital world on estate planning and succession. She lives in Switzerland with her husband Daniel and their twins, Dixie and Trixie. The family is making a collective effort to deplete the Swiss national chocolate reserves – they progress, undaunted by the scale of the task ahead of them.

Part 4 – Believing

Joe Dunthorne

I used to think of tinnitus as something given to me by my favourite bands, the same way they threw their plectrums into the crowd. To come home from the Brixton Academy and for a few hours carry the guitarist's feedback in your ears was a kind of gift. When I started playing in my own band, I still thought of the ringing in my ears as evidence of our total commitment to punk. In a padded rehearsal room near the train station in Norwich, our rhythm guitarist would sneakily turn himself up a notch, which meant that our lead guitarist – sensitive to all threats – would immediately turn himself up a notch, leaving me, the bass player, with my ego-less commitment to equilibrium, to turn myself up a notch and then, of course, turn myself up a *further* notch in anticipation of the others' inevitable responses. And so on and so on, while our drummer just remained horribly, painfully loud. Afterwards I would step from the practice room back into daylight with my head feeling jangly and full, like a piggy bank before it gets smashed with a hammer. The noise in my ears felt satisfying and authentic. It was easy for me to feel that way because I knew the ringing would stop. And for a long time it did.

After my music career ended, I decided I stood a better chance of becoming a writer. I was working in a call centre, encouraging stressed people to consolidate their debts, and in between phone calls I wrote poems and stories for each letter of the phonetic alphabet. A few years later I had finished and sold my first novel and I was writing full time. I had reached that important milestone whereby I no longer found it laughable and pretentious to say, 'My name is Joe, I'm a novelist.' I wrote in my bedroom in my shared flat, but after a while I felt like I needed to be out of the house. 'I think it's just healthy to have a commute,' was the sort of thing I said. I started going to the British Library, more specifically to the Humanities I reading room, which after a while I found too busy, too obvious, and so I moved to Science and then to Rare Books and Music, and then finally to Asian and African Studies. Then I bought an expensive membership to the private London Library in Piccadilly, where I quickly rejected the main reading room and searched out my own little spot among the shelves, a secret desk on the third floor tucked between books on sewage disposal and somnambulism. I hadn't yet noticed it, but there was a direct correlation between success in my career and hypersensitivity to my work environment.

I don't know if you heard, but they turned my novel into a film.

I decided that no library was good enough and I rented my own office space. I liked it because it had a view of a brick wall. Both Zadie Smith and Somerset Maugham have said that great literature can never be written if you have a nice view from your window. Plus I was also near a main road, which allowed me to buy fluorescent industrial earplugs and Bose noise-cancelling headphones. Jonathan Franzen wrote his award-winning novel *The Corrections* while wearing earplugs, headphones and a blindfold. I started getting up as early as I could. I don't know if you've ever procrastinated by reading about successful people's working habits, but it's really effective. Among writers there's a lot of competition about who can say they get up the earliest. It used to be passable to start writing film scripts at nine in the morning, like Ingmar Bergman. Then it was OK to start at eight, like Stephen King. Then came Toni Morrison, at her desk by seven. Then you've got Barbara Kingsolver and Hemingway and Auden, all rising with the dawn. But how can you see the dawn if you don't get up before it? I wanted to be like Nicholson Baker, who wakes at 4.30 a.m. when the mind is 'newly cleansed'.

So I got up in the dark when it was quiet and even the birds were asleep and cycled to my office and put in my earplugs and put on my noise-cancelling headphones and stared hard at the brick wall out my window as light broke across this great city and, now that everything was perfect, I prepared to write my phenomenal masterpiece. Every day I would write a thousand brilliant words before Stephen King had breakfast.

And then fate intervened.

Eeeeeeeeeeeee.

Tinnitus affects 10–15 per cent of the adult population, and it's a serious problem for 1–2 per cent. It varies massively from person to person. For some people it sounds like electricity pylons, for others it sounds like tree frogs or a sizzling frying pan or, for those with pulsatile tinnitus, they hear their heartbeat in the fuzz, like there's an experimental club night taking place, permanently, in the basement of their brain. My noise-cancelling headphones could not cancel this noise because it was coming from inside my head. A noise like a giant licked finger moving round the rim of a giant wine glass.

Each morning when I woke up it was there. Sometimes it went away in the afternoons, or I stopped noticing it, but as soon as I opened my eyes there was an invisible, unkillable fly hovering just beside my ear. At first came denial, checking all the electrical items in the house. Then anger, wanting to tear my ears off. Then depression, sleeplessness, listening to the buzzing, letting myself be swallowed by its strange textures and rhythms. Only much later, thankfully, did I achieve a kind of acceptance. And I'm wary to say this story has a moral. Because I know for many people tinnitus is permanently debilitating, and it can't be thought of – as I am about to suggest – as a helpful way to puncture the creative ego. But in my case at least, the noise inside my skull made my pursuit of the perfect work environment seem ridiculous. So now I work at home. At the kitchen table. I can usually hear my son screaming. It's fine. And when my tinnitus is bad, I just drown it out with music. Although not just any music. I'm still high maintenance, and while I'm working I can't listen to anything that has lyrics – because they would interfere with my word choices – and I can't listen to anything with a clear beat or percussion – because that would interfere with the metrics of my poetry – and I can't listen to anything with a strongly directional melody – because that would be too suggestive of mood – and so what I'm saying is I have discovered there is only one piece of music that I can write to.

It's an ambient song by Aphex Twin called 'Stone in Focus' and it's from the vinyl release of his 1994 album *Selected Ambient Works Volume II*. It's ten minutes long and I like to put it on loop. I love the single rhythmic knocking sound, in the distance, like a clock ticking. As though to say, *Your life is draining away. You will be dead soon. You will be dead soon. Five years is way too long to spend writing a comic novel.* I love the soft synth pads, which make you feel like you're moving up through layers of cloud, the air growing thin as you rise above the drifts of cirrus, through the solar wind, out into the atmosphere, weightless now, watching our blue planet shrink behind you, the sun a single fixed point that in a moment is gone, drifting out through the darkness of the spiral arm, where there is nothing, only emptiness beyond the imagination – and you, you who have been given life, given sentience, you who already wasted hours of the day learning how to play 'Waterloo Sunset' on the acoustic, do you not think you owe it to yourself, owe it to whatever unfathomable stroke of cosmic luck put you in front of a keyboard with ten independently articulate fingers and a brain, do you not think you owe it to the tiny chance of your existence to write your fucking novel?

'Stone in Focus'
Written by Richard D. James
Performed by Aphex Twin
Taken from the album *Selected Ambient Works Volume II*,
released on Warp Records in 1994

YouTube

This story was first performed at Wilton's Music Hall on 30 May 2016.

Joe Dunthorne was born and brought up in Swansea. His debut novel, *Submarine*, was translated into twenty languages and made into an award-winning film. His second novel, *Wild Abandon*, won the Encore Award in 2012. His latest is *The Adulterants*. His first collection of poems, *O Positive*, was published by Faber & Faber in 2019. He lives in London.

Stella Duffy

Kia ora. I was born in a council estate in Woolwich. I'm the youngest of seven kids, and our estate looked out at the Thames back in the days before Woolwich was gentrified. We were on the fourth floor and from the balcony I could hear the ships going down the river.

When I was five we moved back to my dad's native New Zealand. When he was just eighteen, my dad joined the Royal New Zealand Air Force to fight fascism across the world. And here in London he met my mum. After the war they had seven kids because we were working-class people and that's just what working-class people did – to make fun, we make babies. When I was five years old, my mum's parents were dead, and my dad's dad was dead, and my dad's mother was dying. And so we moved back to New Zealand. My mum, who's a south Londoner from Kennington, said goodbye to her five elder children and to everything she knew, this woman aged forty-eight with a one-way ticket to the other side of the world.

We arrived in New Zealand and we moved to a small town which was 70 per cent Māori and Polynesian. And I had the great privilege of growing up in this town that was mostly Māori and Polynesian. It meant that, as a white minority (albeit in a colonised country), I benefited from exposure to all these other cultures. And one of the cultures that I was exposed to most, of course, was Māori culture. And in Māoritanga we would introduce ourselves with this fantastic *mihi*.

I would say, *'Ko Waikato, ko Thames nga awa.'* The Waikato near where I grew up in New Zealand and the Thames are my rivers.

'Ko Pohaturoa, ko Shooters Hill nga maunga.' My mountains are Pohaturoa and Shooters Hill.

'Ko Shaw Saville Southern Cross *te waka.'* My family travelled to New Zealand on the *Shaw Saville Southern Cross*.

'Ko Stella Duffy taku ingoa.'

(I would tell you my name last, after I told you my mountain, my river, our *waka*.)

And for this story, my river – the Thames – matters enormously.

My Kiwi dad taught me to swim in Woolwich Baths.

And my Kiwi dad taught me to swim in the Pacific at night.

And my Kiwi dad taught me to swim in the lakes all around the Waikato River in the middle of the North Island of New Zealand.

And my Kiwi dad was also a violent alcoholic, like a lot of those men who suffered in the war.

My Kiwi dad was all those things – all the good, all the light, all the dark. And I got swimming from him.

When he was thirty-six, my father was diagnosed with testicular cancer. He was treated at St Thomas'. And because it was the sixties, and because it was testicular cancer, he had one testicle removed. Then he was treated with heavy radiation. He was very ill, and because of the radiation, he and my mother didn't expect to have another baby. But then I came along. They called me the miracle baby, but maybe that was just because I was the redhead...

My dad taught me to swim, and he gave me passion and love of the water.

He nearly died when his plane got shot down, and he nearly died when he was thirty-six from testicular cancer.

He eventually died when I was twenty-five. And when I was thirty-six I was diagnosed with breast cancer, with a lump that came up overnight under my right breast. I woke up with it. And because breast cancer doesn't run in my family, because 70 per cent of breast cancers don't run in the family, it took them six weeks to diagnose.

My wife and I were trying to have children at this time with our babyfather. When I said to them at the hospital, 'What's that going to do to my fertility?' they said, 'Well, it won't do any good...'

But then they were really kind and they were really helpful, and they shuffled us off to the fertility unit. Five embryos were made out of the eggs that they wrenched from me. Anyone reading this who's been through the same thing knows that it's bloody painful and it's bloody hard, and you doesn't always get a happy ending.

I went through the cancer, and I had a big surgery and six months of chemo and two months of radiotherapy. My wife got pregnant while I was having radiotherapy, and she miscarried and she never got pregnant again.

Three years later I tried with those five embryos, and they died. One by one in me.

Little swimming things dying one by one.

I kind of thought it was OK. The trade-off was chemo or fertility, and I kind of thought that was OK.

In 2014 I was diagnosed with breast cancer again. Fourteen years later. You know, we who've been through cancer, we talk in terms of fives and tens. I won't be the only cancer patient among those reading this, and I'm not presuming to tell your story, but we talk in terms of fives and tens. When I said this to my consultant, he said, 'Yes, but that's for the statisticians. Our truth is that one day is good. One day.'

It was really hard. In 2014, I was just fifty and I was looking forward to more life – and I am still. But it felt like I'd made this trade-off, except there are no trade-offs.

We know that, right?

There are *no* life trade-offs.

My father-in-law got really ill and he died, horribly, of a cancer that was making him scream in pain. And for those of us who've been ill, I'm sure I'm not the only one who thinks, *Oh shit, I hope that's not me* every time someone else gets sick. I know it's selfish, I know I should be worried for that person. But every time I think, *Shit, I hope that's not me...*

In 2014 I had just established the Fun Palaces campaign with Sarah-Jane Rawlings, and we had 138 places around Britain taking part. These were mostly led by communities in some of the poorest, most 'deprived' parts of Britain, run by these amazing people who have been so fucked over by austerity. But the culture that they create in their own communities is phenomenal. I was so passionate about this project.

All this time I was working on my novel *London Lies Beneath*, which is absolutely my best novel (but don't tell my publisher, because I've published two since), but it is my best novel, and it's about the Thames and it's about the river. And that came out in 2014. And all this time I was sick. I had an eight-hour surgery and then I was in recovery for another eight hours because I bled out. I was really fucking sick. The morning after my eight-hour surgery, this young doctor told me, 'We nearly lost you last night.' I don't think you should tell someone that when they're very poorly.

All this to say it was a really hard year. And throughout this really hard year, because I was healing, I couldn't swim. I couldn't get in the water. I wasn't able to be in the water. The place where I feel safest, and the place where I feel my best.

Around this time my friend Mary told me about her friend Nadia Nervo, a photographer, who was doing this series of photos of women dancing in public.

And I asked Mary to introduce me to her. Which was my way of saying, 'Me, please!'

I went down to the South Bank, to the Thames. I met Nadia. I had my little old iPod. I listened to my music on my earphones. And on the South Bank, that little stretch between the BFI and the National Theatre, I danced.

It was autumn. I'm not a dancer. I love dancing – dancing feels like being in the water to me – but I'm not a dancer.

But I danced for about half an hour with this song on a loop, and Nadia just kept taking photos.

For the first time, probably since my first cancer and since losing all those babies and since all of that loss, I was in my body. I was back in me, and I haven't lost that.

This moment, and this song, reminded me of being alive.

'Nightswimming'
Written by Bill Berry, Peter Buck, Mike Mills and Michael Stipe
Performed by R.E.M.
Taken from the album *Automatic for the People*,
released by Warner Bros in 1993

Apple Music · Spotify

This story was originally told at Wilton's Music Hall on 10 October 2019.

Stella Duffy is an award-winning writer with over seventy short stories, fourteen plays written and devised, and seventeen novels published in fifteen languages. She has worked in theatre for over thirty-five years as an actor, director, playwright and facilitator. She is the co-founder of the Fun Palaces campaign, supporting community-led culture as a catalyst for connection. She is also a yoga teacher and training to be an existential psychotherapist.

Ross Sutherland

The song that changed my life isn't really a song at all. In fact it's the theme tune to *RoboCop*. On the Nintendo GameBoy.

I promise I'm not being facile.

I want to talk about this 'song' because it is very important to me. And it's not just important as an element of nostalgia – there's enough of that out in the world already. I want to talk about this particular song because it taught me an important lesson on how I should make art. And by extension it also taught me how to be a human being. And I know that's a big thing to lay at the door of the theme tune to *RoboCop* on the GameBoy. But in order to get there, I need to set some context. So...

RoboCop came out on the GameBoy in 1990, when I was ten years old. My friend Rich Evans had a GameBoy that he'd bring into school, and sometimes, if we were called into different lunch groups, Rich would let me play on his GameBoy while he ate his lunch. Usually I'd just have to accept whatever cartridge was in the GameBoy and usually, at that time in 1990, it would be *RoboCop*. *RoboCop* the film was an 18 certificate, so I hadn't actually seen it when I first played the video game – not that it mattered, because I loved video games regardless, and also, what kind of back story was really required to enjoy a video game in the 1990s?

The rules were:

- walk to the right,
- keys open doors,
- kill everyone.

That's all you needed to know.

But *RoboCop* on the GameBoy is... well, it's impossible.

The game opens on a city street in Detroit. You are controlling the eponymous robot cop. You walk about four steps down the street. A punk appears in the window above you. He shoots you. You die.

In my schooldays I don't think I was able to last more than ten seconds as RoboCop before being shot in the head. In the game it feels like you should be able to shoot diagonally up to the window. But you can't – you can either shoot sideways or up. So you'd end up doing this jig until the punk who appears at the window puts you out of your misery.

At my peak in 1990 I was killing RoboCop eighty to a hundred times a day.

What could make someone keep playing a game like that – what possible reward could there be for staying at that Sisyphean coal face? Failing and failing, and failing and failing. Day after day after day...

Only the theme tune.

Only that.

Jonathan Dunn's original composition, which plays over the game's opening credits, thus the music you return to every single time you die. That's what. This wonderful piece of eight-bit electronica, so beautiful and uplifting and yet tinged with this deep, deep melancholy.

Ah... It sounds like...

Well, I'll tell you what it doesn't sound like. It doesn't sound like it should be the theme music for *RoboCop*.

The official score, by Basil Poledouris – the one that he wrote for the motion picture – that is appropriately dark and brooding. It actually sounds a lot like the *Terminator* theme tune. It's kind of cold and metallic and ominous. Jonathan Dunn's GameBoy version, on the other hand, is a completely different composition. Dunn's version feels more like a love theme. It's more like the song that would play at RoboCop's wedding, not the song you would use to gee him up for going on the beat.

Personally, I think that this song was designed with a completely different purpose. It's not designed to set the scene. It's not introducing you to the mean streets of Detroit. It's not meant to be heard as a beginning at all.

As I said, the song looped back around every single time that you died, but I don't think it was meant to be heard as an ending either. Ending songs are usually funereal dirges – those sad little ditties that roll over the 'Game Over' credits. What Jonathan Dunn has given us is something else. It's more like the piece of music that you tend to hear in a film between the end of Act Two and the start of Act Three. This is the moment in the film when you've got a group of heroes, and they've been through just about as much as they can take, and every single one of them has been broken; they've all had the things that define them stripped away from them, one by one, but it's still not over yet – there's still one last task ahead of them. Something uncertain still lies in wait in the shadows, the future so terrifying and unknowable that every single instinct is telling the group to turn back. But then, one by one, each member of the group stands and says, 'You know what, if you guys are in, I'm in too.'

And they stand together as friends, because they realise that together they have the strength that each of them lacks alone, and they will sacrifice everything to protect that bond.

I know that's a lot of drama to get out of a very short piece of music that doesn't have any lyrics.

But that's the scene I see in my head. In Joseph Campbell's *The Hero's Journey*, I think this moment gets called 'The Meeting with the Goddess'. It's a moment of spiritual unity, when you're at your deepest, darkest moment. On the story circle, it's the moment that is furthest away from home, but it's also the moment when you start to learn something about who you really are. And when that music plays in *RoboCop* on the GameBoy, it triggers a similar scene in my head.

It makes me think, *Yes, I've just died – and as RoboCop, no less – but I have not failed alone. In fact, millions of other kids have definitely screwed up this video game just as badly as I have. And you know what – if they're still in, then I'm in too...*

I won't let one dead RoboCop drag me off this path of destiny. Because failure isn't what tears us apart. Failure is what brings us together. So, yes, I'll play again. I'll keep fighting. Together until the end...

This is what I find so fascinating about Jonathan Dunn's composition – the song knows that the game is too cruel. So it dramatises failure in an ever-repeating loop, and that makes you, the player, the hero. Not the short-lived robotic cop who only lives for thirty seconds and can't fire diagonally. You the player, you are the central character, you're the person whose trials we are following.

Now, I think this kind of stuff is the most interesting part of video-game design. All games try and solve this problem differently. But the problem is essentially always the same: how can we use failure as a way to spur us on, instead of something that pushes us away?

Because that is not just a video-game problem. That's a life problem. You've got teenagers in school that really struggle staying on a single task for more than a few minutes, who switch off when faced by a new challenge because they're afraid of the unknown. They're afraid of failing. And yet these same kids are going home and then playing the same level of *Call of Duty* for four hours solid, dying over and over and over again, in pursuit of the 100 per cent perfect rendition.

All I'm saying is that I think that sometimes when it comes to failure, there's a lot of stuff that we can learn from video games. There's certainly a lot of stuff I learned from video games.

So the message of this song remains with me. Long after I was separated from its source, I held on to it. I made a mix tape, on cassette, of all my favourite video-game themes, by holding a mic up to the speaker. (We all did that, didn't we?) And what I found out was that every time I was down, whenever I was lonely, whenever I felt that I'd failed, it was the *RoboCop* song that brought me back around. Because, I think, it turned an ending into another act. Another chance to die.

In time I learned to apply this approach to my writing as well. Writing for me became like a game – I would set the rules to a puzzle, and I would try to solve that puzzle. Like writing a poem that only contains one vowel. Or like writing a play that reverses halfway through, like a palindrome. This is how I learned to write. And the trick I found – and I know this sounds counterintuitive – was that I needed to make my word games really, really hard – like cynically and devastatingly unfair. I had to make my writing challenges just as hard as *RoboCop* on the GameBoy. Because if I did this, then the impossible word game would push me to reveal things that I didn't really want to reveal. I would fail so many times, trying to write, that I would stop being afraid of failure, and through that endless process, I might even learn something about myself.

I might even get to meet the Goddess…

I once wrote an hour-long poem that was meant to synchronise, shot for shot, with an old VHS tape that I found in my attic. And it was so hard to write that just through the process of doing it I ended up accepting that I had depression. That was not something I'd ever admitted to myself before that moment. I just needed a game that was hard enough to force out the truth.

Before you listen to the song, I want to dedicate this story to my grandad. Because the night that my grandad died, I went for a walk on my own to process what had happened. I was living in Liverpool at the time and I went for a walk through Sefton Park, and the *RoboCop* theme came on my iPod and I just stopped in the middle of this big Victorian park in the middle of the night, and I listened to it and absorbed it. And I know how stupid this sounds, but it gave me a weird sense of strength. It helped me fold that sadness into a new beginning.

So this is for you, Alec.

Dead or alive, you're coming with me.

The theme from *RoboCop* for the GameBoy, released in 1990
Composed by Jonathan Dunn

YouTube

This story was first performed at The Tabernacle, London, on 20 October 2016.

Ross Sutherland (imaginaryadvice.com) is the writer/producer of the long-running storytelling podcast *Imaginary Advice* (British Podcast Award, Best Fiction Series). His other writing credits include the documentary *Stand By for Tape Back-Up*, BBC2's *Missing Episode* and the palindromic play *Party Trap*.

Alex Romeo

Girl meets boy.

After a few years, they fall in love. A few years after that, they get married. And one month before they celebrate their second wedding anniversary, boy announces he's leaving girl for a person he met three weeks ago.

My knees went first. It was something I'd read about but never thought I'd actually experience in real life. I dry-heaved. Clichés exploded around me like fireworks. And then it was over. Ten years of my life was filed away, negated. Move on. Nothing to see here.

Almost immediately I needed music. I needed a song to absorb and reflect my shock, my immediate depression, my sorrow and my pain back at me. Because at first you don't want to run from it. You might think you want to, but you really don't. You need that emotional mirror, not someone to tell you it's all going to be all right.

In the immediate aftermath of the break-up I lay in bed in silence, trying to make sense of it. I questioned whether I had ever actually been in love or whether I'd just been tricking myself because I *wanted* to be in love. I had thought I was in love. But if he never really loved me, even if I loved him, how could that have been real?

What *is* love?

As if filing for divorce wasn't unpleasant enough, I also got a bonus existential crisis. I was acutely aware that my post-break-up rhetoric sounded like a broken record to my friends. And as much as we all love the Pet Shop Boys, no one wants to hear 'What Have I Done to Deserve This?' on a loop for three years.

I ran away. To Canada, Vancouver Island. In late October. Because I'm a masochist who loves Halloween. I didn't know it yet, but I was on a quest like the knights of yore. My steed was an economy Nissan rental car with a dodgy heater. I was driving down the highway with the sea on one side and the rainforest on the other, listening to Neil Young sing 'Heart of Gold' (because I was in Canada and I presumed it was just what you did). All along the highway were signs saying TSUNAMI WARNING. If a tsunami had struck right then, I'd be dead pretty fast, I thought, because I was so close to the ocean I could see the colour of the surfboards riding the waves.

Suddenly a huge brown bear lumbered into the middle of the road. I screeched to a halt. We were the only two mammals on the road. He was so big, he could easily have munched right through the tiny car to get to me. The bear swung his giant head towards me and we stared at each other. Then he turned towards the rainforest and lolloped casually into the trees.

I pulled off the road and parked by the deserted Pacific shoreline. I stared out at the sea for what felt like hours. The sky was blue, the waves were crashing and there were mountains behind me. A song had been following me around Canada. It's by Sarah McLachlan and it's called 'Elsewhere'. And in it, she sings a line about a place that is heaven to no one else but her. I found a stick on the beach and wrote those lyrics in the sand. An incredible peace descended. Maybe this was it, I thought. Maybe *this* was the perfect song! But it wasn't, was it? I didn't want serenity from a song. My quest was to find a reflection of my pain in music. A surging wave, a wild animal of a song that forced me to look into my heart, a song that said, 'You can let it consume you, or you can scream it out and move on.'

I kept searching.

There are songs to fall in love to and there are songs about lost love. But what happens next? What about songs to help you get up in the morning in the weeks following a break-up? Or songs to soothe you when you wake up on your birthday and for the first time in ten years you realise you're alone? Perhaps a song about how it feels to accidentally make the same amount of dinner as usual and then realise you'll have to eat all of it because risotto doesn't keep well?

I panicked about the future. I wanted to be able to give someone the love that I felt clotting inside me like a jug of cream left out on a hot day. I had to keep telling myself that I *could* love, that I *have* loved, and that I *was* capable of loving again. I was searching for the song that could represent all of that.

I found solace in poetry and film and art as the months went on, but I was yearning for a song that could give me something so personal it seemed impossible. Sympathy. Righteous anger. Confidence. Hope.

As a wronged woman, I was searching for a sister voice that could express not bitterness but triumph. Not in a sneering, contemptible way, but from the viewpoint of moving forward, learning, deserving to love again.

I started listening to Taylor Swift. I listened to 'We Are Never Ever Getting Back Together' so many times, I memorised the spoken part in the middle.

My brother and his girlfriend dragged me to the cinema to take my mind off things. We saw *American Hustle*, which I did *not* like. And not just because Christian Bale makes the least convincing

Jew I've ever seen on screen (and I say that as a genuine – if occasionally unconvincing – Jew myself). One of the subplots of *American Hustle* is that Bale's character is a cheating husband, with his wronged, gaslit wife painted as crazy and irresponsible. How original...

When the film ended, I made some grumpy comments about it and headed off home. But as I pulled into my parking space, I suddenly started crying, unexpectedly triggered by this stupid film. The crying became a howl, and I found myself sitting in my car, screaming and wailing like a wounded animal, with the windows closed, in the dark. I needed something that could be that howl for me, and I hadn't found it yet.

I got desperate and googled 'best break-up songs'. Results suggested that Coldplay's 'The Scientist' is the ultimate break-up song. It isn't.

I plundered my music library. Amy Winehouse, Kate Bush, Fleetwood Mac, Leonard Cohen, Adele. I went rogue with Sondheim and Metallica, and furious with Sinead O'Connor and Tori Amos and PJ Harvey, trying to get my fix.

Joni Mitchell's album *Blue* had accompanied me during my *first* ever heartbreak, so I couldn't go back there. I didn't want to escape down her 'River', or to give the person who had used me and thrown me away, betrayed me and my family, broken every promise he'd ever made and treated me like a villain, the indulgence of being called 'Darling'. It was that simple.

I took an even deeper dive into my music library and rediscovered Damien Rice's 'Rootless Tree', a song so savage I found it hard to listen to when I *was* in a happy relationship. It was a crucial turning point – a ragged chorus that literally howls 'Fuck you and all we've been through'. I thought, *This is it – I've found the song!* And then, in the last chorus, there it was. That *other* four-letter word. The L-word. A word that I couldn't tolerate, right in the middle of this perfect primal scream.

When my divorce came through – a page of A4 with a couple of paragraphs of legalese and a court stamp – I listened to Bob Dylan's 'Don't Think Twice, It's All Right'. There's a little gesture at the end of the track, the suggestion that it was all just a waste of time. It's just so beautifully casual. But it still wasn't the cathartic howl I was looking for. I needed this song to resonate with my heart like a tuning fork.

Nick Cave recently wrote about a phenomenon he calls 'Hiding Songs'. 'Do you ever feel like that about songs,' he wrote, 'that they were designed with you especially in mind, and that no one could ever begin to understand them in the way you do?' He listed ten of his favourites. I just needed one.

By this point, I was pretty sure I'd never find the perfect song. What kind of song could multitask like I was asking it to? Perhaps it hadn't been written yet, I told myself. But part of me knew it already existed. That it was waiting for me to find it.

My hunt continued, and a couple of years later it came to an end, thanks to the shuffle algorithm on my phone. I was on a train, staring out of the window, when a song pinged straight into my soul. It was called 'Seven'. I had heard it many times before, but now I found myself listening with new ears. The lyrics, the melody, the key – everything about this song encapsulated how I felt.

It was as though the song was actually about me, personally. I felt a huge wave of relief. I knew that this was my Hiding Song. And I knew I could come back to it as many times as I'd need to.

Jamie Lawson is an artist I had stumbled across nearly twenty years previously, in a tiny room above a pub in Camden. Jamie is a singer-songwriter who achieved something I'd never seen before – he silenced an entire room of drinkers with his music. And you really could hear a pin drop. I was blown away by his intensity and passion and became a lifelong fan that night. After a few years I got to know him personally. (Jamie got the breakthrough he deserved when he was signed by Ed Sheeran, and I am so thrilled to watch him go from strength to strength.)

It's worth saying that I've never discussed the lyrics of 'Seven' with Jamie. I'd heard him sing it live many times, but it had never resonated with me at this level. My interpretation is that it is a song about a person betrayed in love; it's an inspirational song that says exactly what I needed to hear. It's sympathetic but not pitying; it's triumphant without being gloating. It's about hope and the future, and it's not bitter. It celebrates endurance and strength.

It seems to tell me, 'You're a good person. You persevered through a terrible time, but you'll be OK. And you deserve to be happy.'

And I am.

'Seven'
Written by Jamie Lawson
Performed by Jamie Lawson
Taken from the album *The Pull of the Moon*, released on
Lookout Mountain in 2010

Apple Music   Spotify

This story was first performed at Omeara London on 13 January 2019.

Alex Romeo spends most of her time in theatres, working to make shows accessible for deaf and hard-of-hearing audiences in her roles as a captioner and access consultant. She is an occasional scribbler, amateur photographer and professional redhead.

Dan Kieran

When I was four, I played the violin. I started at a young enough age to get good pretty quickly. I could play by ear, so I knew instinctively if a note was wrong. I had a teacher called Mr Chittock, who I would have done anything for. He taught the Suzuki method, which, as any of you who have come across it will know, is all about intuition and fun. He told me things like, 'You don't play with your fingers, you play with your heart,' which almost makes me weep to remember thirty-seven years on. If I have a life philosophy, that is where it came from.

I'm not sure how good I was, but I do know I loved it, and music was something that seemed to flow out of me. I can still recite the notes of the first piece I learned, called 'Allegro': 'A, A, E, E, F, G, A, F, E, E, D, D, C, C, B, A, B, C, A.'

My mum says I got a scholarship to the Wells Cathedral School, but she and Dad didn't want me to board so I didn't go. Playing the violin gave me a way to communicate how I felt before I really knew that was what I was doing. It was the first time I felt the power of expressing myself through art. I got lost playing my violin. I also know that I loved Mr Chittock. It was the first time I'd loved someone who was not a member of my family. I loved him as you can only love a teacher who opens up your conscious experience of the world.

I started doing yoga because he said it would be good for my music. So, at four years old, I was dropped off at the local sports centre by my mum to do yoga on a Wednesday night, wearing my SuperTed leg warmers and carrying a scratchy towel, performing the positions with a room full of what I recall as old ladies, who were probably in their twenties and thirties. More than once I fell asleep in the lotus position because my spot on the thickly woven yellow carpet was in front of a radiator. I remember lipstick smiles and my hair being stroked to wake me up. I was out of place, which I've learned over the years is the only place I've ever truly felt at home.

I think everyone has a special power. Something they can do without thinking. And when you are in tune with this part of yourself, everything else makes sense. Music was it for me. It was bliss. I worked hard at playing because it wasn't work at all. But my music lessons, and my use of music to express what I felt in my head and my heart, came to a very abrupt end. Mr Chittock died.

He used to teach me in this little building next to an old oak tree in my primary school. It had lots of windows, so it was always very warm inside, with sunbeams darting through the branches and panes of glass like the sticks in Kerplunk. I still remember the Christmas-morning feeling washing over me whenever the blinds were up and I knew he was in there, teaching. I was always so excited walking up the steps for my lessons with my little case.

But one day I was told he had gone and our lessons were over. The blinds were down that day and every day after. I remember looking at the closed blinds during playtime each day, wondering where he'd gone and why he hadn't said goodbye. I didn't realise I was too heartbroken to be cross, and it has taken years to fathom the emptiness it created inside me. You see, no one told me he had died. I suppose they wanted to protect me, so they just said he had gone. At the time, then, I knew nothing about his death. I just knew that he'd left and that without him I couldn't seem to play any more. So I stopped.

New music teachers came and went but the music in my heart had left with him. I had no explanation for the absence and I grew to hate my quarter-size violin. Holding it felt like cradling something rotten and dead. I remember crying and twisting the bow until it splintered, hiding the pieces under my bed.

I struggled with music after that. It was like I couldn't let it 'in' without intense effort. I still can't lose myself in music as easily as other people can. Or at least I couldn't until I discovered the music of the person who wrote and performed this song. Even now, if I'm at a party, it takes a lot to get me to dance. Unless his music comes on. And then, even if no one else is dancing, I do.

I suppose the narrative I have told myself, which I have come to believe and use to define who I am, is that I will never be able to express myself in writing in the way I used to with my violin. That chance is gone. I'll spend my life writing in the hope that I might be able to use words one day in the way I used music back then. But I also know I have the ability to spot it in the music, and other kinds of craft, of other people, which is now what excites and motivates me.

But ten years after I stopped playing, I found a song that not only had come from the state of mind, or perhaps artistic connection, I had felt playing music but also, and this is why I found it so astonishing, because it reached from the mind of the artist into mine with seemingly no interference or friction.

I'm convinced that we all know who we are, what matters to us, what excites us and what moves us. We know it in our minds and in our bones with frustrating clarity. I say frustrating, because in our minds we are alone, cut off from the world we inhabit emotionally and literally. The great opportunity and tragedy of being alive is that we are unable to communicate this self-knowing to ourselves and other people in a way they and we can understand. So we translate our feelings into thoughts using words, which can be clumsy and rarely reflect what we feel inside. We show it in our life choices, which can be even more mystifying, and in the friendships we cultivate. We try and reflect it, or experience it wordlessly, in the work and art of others and ourselves. Our lives are spent attempting to be known. In my own life, when I feel I have failed, that failure is always rooted in a failure to be understood.

This song was the first time a work of art bridged the gap between my mind and another. My Roberta Flack moment. The fact that the song also tackles the nature of mortality – and I heard it at the time I was first grappling with my own – meant I couldn't actually listen to it all the way through. I had to lift the needle off the record and take a deep breath because it was too intense to cope with. He sings with a whisper at the start of the song but to me, those first few times, it was deafening.

The philosopher Boethius wrote that there are moments of perfection you experience in life, and in these moments of perfection you glimpse eternity. In those moments you see with the eyes of God. And you gasp. This is what I think Boethius meant. Moments of perfect sight. Perhaps, even, truth. It was as though I had stumbled on a secret that horrified and reassured me I knew I could never explain.

You know the moment when you realise you have forgotten a dream, but the feeling it gave you is still there in your mind? You try and pull the memory of the dream back to be able to feel the feeling more deeply, but the words you need to remember the dream have gone. Then, agonisingly, the feeling goes too, and all you remember is its absence. That's not quite what I mean, but it's the closest the words I have will let me get. This song makes me feel like that, anyway. Sort of.

Prince, who wrote and performed the song, became my way back into music when I was about fourteen. His Nude Tour at Wembley Arena was my first ever live concert. I went with my friend Henry, who was a member of the fan club, so we got seats a few rows from the front. Seeing Prince as your first live gig is the literal definition of the phrase 'a tough act to follow'. That concert was the first time since I played the violin I'd been able to completely lose myself in music. It was the first time I ever danced as a self-conscious teenager too.

When Prince died, friends I hadn't seen in years texted to see if I was OK. Henry and I had a not-very-manly chat on the phone. It took me multiple listens of the *Purple Rain* album over the next few weeks to be able to hear it without getting upset. I'm not trying to hoist myself onto the league table of most heartbroken Prince fans. I mention this because I think I was crying for Mr Chittock, and myself too. All over the world people like me were weeping for the experiences in their lives that his music had played a part in. Because music wasn't something he did. It was something he *was*, and it is something in all of us too. He was a master at communicating the human condition, crossing the bridge from his consciousness to our own. We're all artists, you see. Playing life. Not with our bodies, but with our hearts.

I saw Prince lots of times over the years, and even when he was a bit odd, and he was odd a lot, he was better than everyone else I've seen.

Watching Prince play over the years was always like checking in with my fourteen-year-old self. Reminding me who I was and who I had become. I got older. He didn't seem to. I learned in the time since I first heard this song that the closer you get to facing your mortality, the less frightening it is. I'm less daunted now than I was at fourteen, anyway, which takes the edge off the beautiful panic this song drew from me when I first listened to it back then. Listening to it now is like that moment when you try and remember a dream. I can't remember how I felt those first few times I heard it, but I can remember the delicious life-affirming feeling it created inside me.

If Prince played in the UK, I usually went. But he never played this song. Not for me, anyway. Then he announced a series of shows to be performed in the round at the O2 Arena. They were typically astonishing.

And one night, the last of the seven nights I went, long after most people had gone home and the lights were up – a sign in every other live show I've been to that the night is over – he came out and did an encore. Everyone around me moved to empty seats closer to the stage, but I didn't want to break the spell. I wasn't in a great place in my life at the time. I was dragging a chasm of sadness around me like a shadow no one else could see. I really needed something. Could he? Would he?

He sat at the piano, twinkled with the impish grin I will have in my mind as long as I live and played the song that chose me. It was the one and only time I ever saw him play it.

Rather poignantly, he didn't play it all. But he played enough for me to experience a lump in my throat that morphed into cathartic glee. This song. His song. My song.

'Sometimes It Snows in April'
Written by Prince and Wendy & Lisa
Performed by Prince and the Revolution
Taken from the album *Parade*, released by Warner Bros in 1986

Apple Music   Spotify

This story was first performed at Wilton's Music Hall on 23 February 2017.

Dan Kieran is the author of many books, including *The Surfboard*, *The Idle Traveller*, *Three Men in a Float* and *I Fought the Law*, and he co-edited the infamous *Sunday Times* bestseller *Crap Towns*. He is also co-founder and CEO of the award-winning publishing platform Unbound, the publisher of this fine book.

Cash Carraway

Top five songs to die to.

In at Number 5 we've got... 'Chinese Rocks'.

But – it's got to be the Johnny Thunders and the Heartbreakers version.

It's a murder... *obviously*.

A bloody bludgeoning in a sordid location.

It really is the most perfectly *precise* three minutes of pop-punk to be murdered to.

You'd most probably need my dental records to identify me.

Parts thrown in bin bags.

But what a song to be chucked from the world with.

I don't trust anyone who hasn't thought about what song they'd want to get murdered to. Do you?

Number 4. I could die to... Paul Westerberg's 'World Class Fad'. I could get with that. The underrated 'former Replacements front man' would be blasting through my headphones as I sauntered the streets arrogantly like I do when his music's in my ear.

Well, it would have to be a funny death...

Little bit of back story: I escaped the south London suburb of

Penge at the age of eighteen. The bus dropped me north of the river and I walked a little bit west. Never looked back. It is a sentence of pride to reveal I've never once returned. Not even the lure of a funeral buffet or unlimited hen-night drinks could take me back those ten miles and across that bridge.

This is how it would happen: I'd be strutting along the street, and the 176, destination Penge brazenly emblazoned across its front, would come out of nowhere and knock me down. That'll teach me for turning my back on my roots. And of course, to make matters worse, I'd be trapped underneath it... for *hours*. Not a particularly funny death for me, but it would be for anyone who knows me. They'd chuckle. 'What a way to die. Death by Penge.'

Number 3. A serious one now. 'The 2 of Us' by Suede. That beautiful piano-led masterpiece from *Dog Man Star*. If you're fading away to a soundtrack of Suede, then you're going down the prolonged death route. This ain't no joke. Your demise has been dragging on and on. The family have been waiting for you to go for months now. It's a cancer, *probably*. You were given six months to live over eighteen months ago now and you've been watching everyone mourn you for the past year. Funeral arranged, coffin bought and everyone's like – 'Just get on with it, we've got lives to live here!' and then... one night, the people I love the most, they gather around the morphine tubes and stare at my thin dry lips as I start to whisper my over-rehearsed and *profound* final statement –

Number 2. It's got to be *The Holy Bible* by the Manic Street Preachers. The whole fucking album on repeat, four, five times over. I'm thinking a terrorist-type situation.

I'd find a hiding place. In an air vent above a toilet or something. Yeah. And I'd put the album on to block out whatever crazy shit was happening out there – and from the opening lines of 'Yes' would resign myself to death. And it would be on repeat. Until the phone battery ran out. Then. Perfect timing – explosion. Or gun to the head.

Gone.

It's so important to have the right music playing as you die. Imagine dying to Coldplay. There are actually people out there who have died listening to Coldplay.

Or some shit 'dance music'.

Or Travis. Or Shed Seven.

How did these people *ever* live with themselves?

Number 1 in my top five songs to die to: It's 'The French Inhaler' by Warren Zevon.

It could only be a suicide.

The perfect suicide song.

I took the record out the sleeve and placed it on the turntable. I took the first handful of pills and knocked them back with a red wine. A Malbec. Then the second lot.

I shot them down.

It was... that November, that desolate November of 2018, so grim and – I was... *done.*

Done with it all.

Just worn out.

That November I was living on this estate in Marden, in Kent. Marden is a Coldplay record. No, no – Marden is a Shed Seven reunion tour. Sixteen small venues in minor towns where all the groupies are in their fifties. Marden is forty-five miles south of Penge, which makes it officially fifty-five miles from civilisation.

I was in isolation, cleansed from London, trying to write this book I'd been given a deal for... but hope was playing truant from my heart.

From the lino kitchen floor, I called an old friend.

'I'm playing "The French Inhaler",' I told him.

He knew what that meant.

'It's a good song to die to,' he said.

Then he said, 'Hey, remember when my mum died back when we were at uni and after the funeral we flew over to Los Angeles to see Paul Westerberg play at the Henry Fonda – because he never plays in England – and we checked into that hotel right opposite the Greyhound station on Cahuenga Boulevard, and then we went and got drunk in the Frolic Room (because we'd heard that's where Bukowski drank every night) and then we went to see Westerberg, and you said it was the best gig you'd ever seen, and afterwards the security guard invited us backstage – because he said he liked your accent – and backstage we nervously hung around for a bit and we drank the free beer and chain-smoked as you worked up the courage to speak to Paul so you could ask if we could have a photograph with him and, remember, as the photo was taken you made sure you were dragging on a ciggy so that you'd look cool, but in hindsight it makes you look a bit ridiculous, like you're *trying* to be cool – like people who wear sunglasses indoors, right? – and the next day we had tickets to *The Late Late Show with Craig Ferguson* because Paul Westerberg was a guest to promote *Folker*, and we were sat in the audience, and Paul and the bass player spotted you, and they made a big deal about waving at you, like they couldn't believe that this young girl from London would be so in love with their music that she'd travel halfway around the world to see them live. And then a few hours later we literally bumped into him on Hollywood Boulevard when we were on the way to see the second Henry Fonda show and, "Cash!" he shouted down the street, and then he greeted us like long-lost friends. And they say never meet your idols, but Paul Westerberg was quite literally the perfect gentleman and he said, "Hey, you travelled all the way from London, you're coming in with me," and he poured us red wine, remember? And just before he went on stage, he asked if there was a song you wanted him to play that night and you said, "Yeah, actually there is," and you asked if he could play "If Only You Were Lonely", and he said, "Sure, Cash. I'll play that song for you." He rarely plays that song live. And halfway through the show Westerberg suddenly got serious and he said, "This song is for my friends from London." And he played "If Only You Were Lonely", and you know what, I actually have it on bootleg somewhere, you should listen to it some time, and remember, after the show it was really surreal because he introduced us to Lucinda Williams, who I suspect he was having an affair with, and he introduced us to Prince's drummer and... the man from the Rembrandts, he introduced us to the man from the Rembrandts, the guy who wrote the theme tune to *Friends*. And were so happy that night.'

'Yeah, I remember. I remember all that,' I said.

'You were living. You did that because you were living. You were living life in that honest way you do. Most people are afraid to truly live, Cash, but you travelled across the world to tell a faded rock star how much their music means to you. People are afraid to be honest because they're worried they'll look foolish or be mocked. And yes, honest people are inevitably ridiculed, but not because they're foolish; it's because it scares the type of people who make the bad choices and attend Gary Barlow concerts and shit like that.

'And it's been difficult to live the way you've had to live these past few years, but you have a book deal – a way out of poverty. A way to live again. And you're going to die one day, yes, but not like this. You can't die like this. Not tonight. You're not going to die in a flat in Kent. How embarrassing, Cash. You could have the terrorist situation listening to the Manics, or be murdered to Johnny Thunders.'

What the actual fuck, Cash? Who are you?

'How about a song to live to? You need to start thinking about songs to live to!

'OK. Now, put your fingers down your throat, that's it. That's it. Spew it all up...'

And I vomited. And as I vomited, he sang it. My friend sang it to me. As I puked to not die, he sang the whole song for me. Just like Paul Westerberg did.

A song to stay alive to.

'If Only You Were Lonely'
Written by Paul Westerberg
Performed by the Replacements
Taken from the album *Sorry Ma, Forgot to Take Out the Trash*,
released on Twin/Tone in 1981

Apple Music   Spotify

This story was first told at the Sage Gateshead, as part of the Words Weekend Festival on 7 December 2019.

Cash Carraway (www.cashcarraway.com) is an award-winning writer. Her first book, *Skint Estate*, was published in 2019 and became a word-of-mouth sensation. She's been commissioned by the Clean Break Theatre Company, Battersea Arts Centre, the Royal Court, the Old Vic and Soho Theatre. Her second book, *Flesh Pot*, will be published in 2022.

Adam Shakinovsky

The story of the song that changed my life starts – like any genuinely moving story – with some incredibly tenacious haemorrhoids.

It's August 2012, the height of the London Olympic Games. My wife Elizabeth and I are expecting our first child in two weeks' time. At the start of the year we'd found out that she was pregnant and I'd decided I was going to lose some weight. So I started eating lean and exercising regularly – cycling, Pilates, t'ai chi – and it worked. Slowly but surely, I'd started to lose weight. One to two pounds a week. My shirts had started to billow out around me like a kite, and my trousers were just as baggy, practically falling off.

And now, just as I'm getting down to my ideal weight, I've got these bloody haemorrhoids.

As I go to see the GP, Elizabeth says, 'Just mention to them that you've lost a lot of weight.'

And I'm like, 'Well, yeah, I've been mentioning it to everyone! Of course I'm going to tell the doctor!'

The GP in question is freshly qualified. Very earnest and professional.

She says to me, 'Mr Shakinovsky, kindly remove your jeans and lie down on your side for me, facing the wall.'

'Of course, Doctor.'

I lie down, but before she has the opportunity to say, 'Now I'm going to insert a finger into your rectum...' she inserts her finger into my rectum.

I yelp.

Not a cute puppy yelp, or like I fell into a cold puddle. No. More like a high-pitched, cartoon-like, Goofy-falling-three-miles-off-a-cliff sort of sound.

Outside the doctor's office, feet halt in the corridor, the chatter in the reception stops, and I'm pretty sure I've stunned London into stilled silence.

We both hurriedly try to make each other feel better.

'I'm so sorry, Mr Shakinovsky! I realise I didn't give you enough warning before insertion.'

'No, *I'm* sorry, Doctor. I don't normally make that type of sound.'

After a hasty urine test I bundle myself out of the door. But by the time I get out of the Underground on my way to work she calls my mobile.

'In all the embarrassment I forgot to give you a blood test. There's some protein in your urine, so please get back here when you can.'

I'm with the GP again, now with Elizabeth.

The doctor approaches looking a little stricken.

'Your blood sugar is at twenty-five. It should never really be higher than six or seven. You need to get to A & E as soon as you can. I've called ahead to Chelsea and Westminster. They're expecting you. Please go now, as quickly as you can.'

I don't know if you've ever spent a long time waiting in a hospital, but it feels a lot like sitting in an aeroplane with flight attendants going back and forth. But instead of peanuts, drinks and duty free, people bring me increasingly confusing, and increasingly bad, news.

A doctor with his head slightly bowed says, 'Mr Shakinovsky, just to let you know that your HBA1C is at 125. It isn't supposed to go above forty. We're putting you on an insulin drip and we'll keep monitoring you.'

I say, 'My HBA1-what-now?'

A short while later a nurse approaches, leaning down with her hand on my shoulder. 'Mr Shakinovsky, to make you aware, we're currently treating it as if it's type one diabetes. It can be managed somewhat if you find a balance between your carbohydrates and NovoRapid, in combination with a strong basal like glargine or Levemir.'

'OK...'

Later still, another doctor arrives, squatting down to my level. Now I'm picking up on a theme. As the news gets worse, the bearers of it seem to get lower and lower down to deliver it.

'To give you some more information on the condition. Statistically speaking, it is likely that you will have ten to twenty years shaved off your life expectancy, and you're five times more likely to have a stroke, go blind and/or lose a limb.'

'Thank you, Doctor.'

The London sky turns orange before I have another visitor.

Another doctor, now on bended knee.

'You can't go home. We need to keep you here. We don't know how long for. Visiting hours are over and your wife needs to leave.'

'...'

Elizabeth says goodbye and the sun goes down. They put me in a wheelchair and take me to a different ward for the night. When I say ward... if I'm Ebenezer Scrooge in *A Christmas Carol*, this ward is the Spirit of Hospital Visits Future. It is filled with old guys in really bad shape. There's plenty of coughing, rattling, rasping breaths. The sick call out in half-sleep and half-nightmares.

As I take it all in, I realise I'm sweating all over. My hands, my legs, my whole back and front are drenched. I'm dizzy, weak and... woozy.

Just as the world starts to slip out of focus, a figures passes my bed. I think it's a nurse, and I mutter as loudly as I can, 'Excuse me... I think something's wrong...'

She checks my blood sugar and soon there are more people there, breaking open tubes of gel and rubbing them into my gums. Ten or fifteen minutes later, she checks again and is happy that I've sufficiently recovered.

I'm still woozy, but I hear my nurse say to her colleague as she rounds the corner, 'It's a good thing he caught me, otherwise he'd be dead now.'

I think about this. I think about Elizabeth, at home in our flat. Pregnant. We've invited a life into this world.

And she's going to be here so soon.

I start to think about the years potentially taken off my life. Can I do all the things I want to do as a dad? Am I going to get to do half the things I *need* to do? What might I miss? Will I be there to help her fix the things that break? Will I be there to help her get up when she falls down? To turn her tears into laughter throughout all the years to come, when it matters most? What if she gets stuck or scared? What if she feels truly lost and calls out for me? And I'm not there?

These thoughts run around my head until I think that despite my exhaustion, I'm never going to sleep again.

Then I take out my phone and put my earphones in. I search through songs until I land on one called 'The Auld Triangle'. I've heard it before and I know that there's something about the way the Clancy Brothers and Tommy Makem harmonise the chorus that calms me. I play it again. And I must play it ten times, twenty times on repeat, until I can feel myself start to breathe properly again. My shoulders relax, my fists unclench and my chest rises and falls. My limbs start to feel heavy at last. And even though I can't answer any of the questions I've just been asking, I fall asleep. Gratefully.

The diagnosis is confirmed, and a few days later I'm released from hospital. Shortly after that, Elizabeth gives birth to Molly Grace Shakinovsky. At that moment Molly creates a mother and a father. And she's perfect.

But she won't sleep!

She screams, she balls up her fists and she fights the feeling until she goes red. And we are trying *everything*. Rocking, shushing, lullaby music, white noise, brown noise, pink noise, a hairdryer. Nothing works.

So, in desperation I pick her up and start to sing 'The Auld Triangle'.

By the end of the first verse I realise that this really isn't helping. At all. I'm not sure she can even hear it over her cries, but I'm out of other ideas. So I keep going.

During the second verse, it's clear that she can hear *something*, and she's looking around for the origin of the sound.

By the third verse she looks directly at me. She sees that I am there. That she is not alone. She stares vigilantly, and her cries subside into more of a gentle sob.

By the end of the fourth verse, her fists relax. Her breaths become shallow as her eyes close. She is asleep in my arms, dreaming of who knows what.

And this becomes the tune I get her to sleep with. It happens more quickly each time. But even if she drifts off after the first or second verse, I always finish it.

Partly I do so in the hope that she drifts down into deeper sleep and sweeter dreams.

But I also do it for me. Because this song is changing my life – by helping me believe that I'm going to keep having one.

I still don't have any of the answers to the questions I asked myself in that hospital bed. But as I sang to her that first time, as I still sing to her now, I leap into a future when her toys might break, when she might fall down, or when her tears might need drying. And this song makes me feel that in the times to come, when it matters most, I'm going to be there.

'Royal Canal (The Auld Triangle)'
Traditional folk song
Performed by the Clancy Brothers
Taken from the album *The Best of The Clancy Brothers
and Tommy Makem*, reissued by Sony Music in 2002

Apple Music   Spotify

This story was first performed at Wilton's Music Hall on 15 February 2018.

Adam Shakinovsky is a storyteller and co-producer of *OneTrackMinds*. When he isn't manfully chopping wood or even more manfully drinking tea, he writes and produces documentaries, podcasts, films, television and children's books. He lives in Surrey with his wife Elizabeth, daughter Molly and son Toby, nestled among a herd of royal deer.

Acknowledgements

OneTrackMinds came into existence after Kristian spent a few months living in Sweden, when he listened to an inordinate number of podcasts – specifically *Desert Island Discs* and *The Moth*. So thanks are due, firstly, to the creators of those two brilliant shows – in particular *DID*'s Roy Plomley (unarguably the finest interviewer who ever lived), Kirsty Young and *The Moth*'s George Dawes Green.

Thanks, too, to Gunilla Molund, who let Kristian and his wife Zoe stay in her home for that Swedish summer, and for inadvertently creating the environment for our show to be born.

If it weren't for the ambition and encouragement of Prasanna Puwanarajah, *OneTrackMinds* may well have never become anything other than yet another one of Kristian's ideas that he bores people's ears off about but never actually does anything with (there are a lot of those). Instead, thanks to P's enthusiasm – and his friendship with the brilliant Holly Kendrick (of whom more in a moment) – *OneTrackMinds* became a proper bona fide live theatre show, put on for the benefit of an audience. Thanks so much to him for helping us to open up our horizons so fruitfully.

If Prasanna is the godfather of the show, then Holly Kendrick is our fairy godmother. She took a punt on Kristian's somewhat amateur pitch for the show (literally, 'Er... interesting people tell a story about a song that changed their life... in some way... on stage... for an hour or so?') and gave us our break – two consecutive nights in May 2016. And, even after Kristian had utterly failed to grasp the concept of what producing a live theatre show involved (an example – he forgot to do any sort of marketing for the show until about two weeks beforehand), she let us come back, again and again and again... And now we won't leave. Holly, thank you for your trust in us and your support for our show.

Huge thanks too to the amazing team at Wilton's – specifically Ryan Funnell, Jake Hughes, Kate Mullan, Lani Strange, Ross Bonny-Hodges, Harry Hickmore and Cath Bates. An extra special shout-out to the wonderful Ellie Standeven, and her just-as-wonderful army of front-of-house helpers; to Michael Lee-Wooley, the most patient man we know, who has tech-produced many of our shows at Wilton's with great humour and efficiency, and to the lovely Rye Milligan, who has stepped in on occasions and been just as brilliant. Oh, and to Rupert, Wilton's besequinned box-office hero, who always cheers us up.

Can we thank a building as well? Is that mad? Perhaps. But *OneTrackMinds* certainly wouldn't be what it is without Wilton's Music Hall. It's simply the most magical theatre in London, if not the entire world, and we knew from the first moment we stepped into the lobby that it was the perfect place for our show. Now it feels like home every time we go back there. We love you, Wilton's, and can't wait for our next visit.

Here's a good place to say a big thank you to Dee McCourt and Molly Hunt at Borkowski, who have been brilliant friends of the show in supporting our publicity and marketing. Thanks too to the team at JHI – especially Joe Kelly, Aimee White, Laura Thomson and Jo Hutchinson – for all your help in building our profile over the years.

We want to – and will – thank all of the brilliant guests who have told a story on our show, but before we do, a few special thank yous. Firstly to our first guests over those two nights in May 2016 – Jemima Foxtrot, Pete Brown, Robert Bound, Jonathan Margolis, Christian Lee, Helen Zaltzman, Joe Dunthorne, Lucy Trodd, Prasanna Puwanarajah, Steven Camden, David Quantick and Erica Buist. All twelve of you bravely accepted our invitation to tell a story about a song that changed your life with absolutely nothing to go on, and in doing so helped make *OneTrackMinds* the show that it is. (And an extra-special shout-out to Jemima for going first.)

Joe Dunthorne helped us to see the value of ensuring that we pay all of our guests a fee (even if it *is* a small one). Robert Bound helped us publicise the show by inviting us on to Monocle Radio. Lucy Trodd offered enormous encouragement ahead of those first shows – especially in urging Kristian to take up the challenge of hosting the thing – and has let us use the brilliant picture of her leading an audience singalong to the Carpenters' 'Goodbye Love', arms spread wide in joyous celebration, in many of our subsequent marketing campaigns.

When we first launched the show, we leaned heavily on the creative genius of the one and only Rob Butcher, who designed our wonderful logo and posters, and helped imbue the whole show with a spirit of excitement and downright hipster coolness.

Thanks to Tessa Reed, who took photos for us on those first nights and at many subsequent shows as well. And to her madly talented daughter Miranda Reed, who created the portraits of each of our contributors throughout this book.

We also want to thank the teams at the other venues we've played the show at – firstly the Tabernacle in Notting Hill, where we did two

179

shows in October 2016, and then the team at Omeara, in particular Chloe Mitchell and latterly Jack Dedman, for encouraging us to use their brilliant venue as the home for our *Hidden Tracks* shows.

Jo Sawicki came to see one of our shows in 2017, and then went out of her way to connect us to her brilliant network, including introducing us to the team at the House of St Barnabas. Thanks to that connection we made one of our dearest friends – the one and only Jenny Barley, who has done so much to support our show, including allowing us to host a very special choir show at the House – of which more shortly...

We've had a lot of fun taking the show on the road to other venues and festivals, and owe a debt of thanks to those who have enabled that to happen – most especially to Linda Ross and her brilliant team at WOMAD, where we've done three hugely enjoyable festival shows. Thanks to Mark Shayler for inviting us along to the Good Life Experience, and for introducing us to the wonderful Charlie Gladstone and his brilliant team. And to Beth Gallimore of Fane Productions, who invited us to take part in the first ever Words Weekend festival up in Gateshead in December 2019. When the world gets back to normal again, we can't wait to take the show to these festivals once more.

Now then, to our storytellers, without whom the show would literally be nothing more than a weirdly curated disco. Thank you to all of you for taking part and opening up a little bit of your soul. You have all been amazing. In addition to those first twelve named above, thank you to (in order of appearance) Charlie Dark, Pippa Evans, Ross Sutherland, Dame Evelyn Glennie, Ian Bruce, Lemn Sissay, Jane Bussman, Neil Hughes, John Robins, Professor John Sutherland, Sylvia Patterson, Francesca Beard, Stuart Heritage, Keith Kahn-Harris, Jason Solomons, Natalie Haynes, James Wheale, Dan Kieran, Molly Naylor, Bill Griffin, Nikesh Shukla, Ruth Bratt, Charlie

Lyne (aka Shackleton), Geoff Deane, Jenn Offord, Antosh Wojcik, Guy Pratt, Harry Michell, Tulip Siddiq MP, Mark Thomas, Deborah Frances-White, Rachel Long, Catherine Mayer, Debris Stevenson, Bompas and Parr, Jay Rayner, Dorit Chrysler, Mark Lewney, Chris Gifford, Chloe Combi, Claire Gordon-Webster, Janet Kay, Blair Mowat, Robert Popper, Jen Moss, Omar Robert Hamilton, Stephen Woolley, Liela Moss, David Saxby, Peter Tatchell, Jessie Buckley, Steve Pretty, Daniel Glaser, Murray Lachlan-Young, Simon Napier-Bell, Piers Torday, Chiara Ventura, Sofie Hagen, Chris Lintott, Ross Lee, Barry Adamson, Iain Cooper, Andy Nyman, Bridget Minamore, Cariad Lloyd, Jon Morter, Sarah Benetto, Michael Horovitz, Josie Lawrence, Richard McDougall, Simon Raymonde, Inua Ellams, Janine Harouni, Nick Shakinovsky, Helen Fleming, Andrew Nolan, Rosa Dachtler, Nicholas Jessup, Dom Fitch, Dara McGarry, Hannah Rodger, Harriet Allner, Cordi Walsh, Jess Nicks, Chibundu Onuzo, Bobby Fitzgerald, Taylor Glenn, Stephen Leslie, Steve Ali, Katie Elliot, Harriet Braine, Shelley Von Strunckel, Kristy McLeod, Haresh Patel, Rob Watt, Alex Romeo, Imogen Deller-Evans, Alice Martin, Katie O'Brien, Tania Shakinovsky, Lucy Czaplizcka, Lara Mitchell, Daniel Cayford, Joseph Baker, Caleb Femi, Tom Basden, Elvis McGonagall, James Ball, Soweto Kinch, Shazia Mirza, Carrie Grant, Mark Shayler, Nell Stevens, Joan Iyiola, James Murphy, Tracy Rakira, Pauline Eyre, Helen Betham, Jacob Micigovsky, Ian Bonar, Taylor Hotvet, Janice Johnson, George Burton, Kemah Bob, Rufus Wright, Chloe Petts, Viv Groskop, Mark Dolan, Patrick Gale, Bec Hill, Luke Turner, Yomi Sode, Dan Clark, Vanessa Kisuule, Kate Spicer, Eley Williams, Ngaio Aniya, Derek Owusu, Rebecca Tantony, Tim Fitzhigham, Amanda Blainey, Joel Golby, Maria Shehata, Kerry Shale, Amrou Al-Kadhi, Adam Meggido, Amber Millington, Rebecca Tanner-Rolf, Daniel-Konrad Cooper, Igor Degtiarev, Roger Grech, Felicity Cloake, Dylan Jones, David Grant, James Sills, Jane Horrocks, Justin Adams, Emma

Purshouse, Jim Al-Khalili, Soumik Ditta, Hilary Gallo, Charlie Gladstone, Katie Melua, Tim McInnerny, Helen Lederer, David Suchet, Adah Parris, Steve Chapman, Ian Bonar, James Wallman, Fred Deakin, Stella Duffy, Brenda Gilhooly, Rhik Samadder, Karen Krizanovich, Katie Puckrik, Freya Mallard, Daniel Rachel, Julian Knox, Polly Bennett, Ingrid Oliver, Cash Carraway, Malik Al-Nasir and David Olusoga.

(Phew.)

There are a couple of people we need to single out from that line-up. First, Deborah Frances-White, who, having told three different stories at *OneTrackMinds* shows over the years, is our most prolific storyteller, and has also blessed us with the honour of writing the foreword to this book. Other multiple storytellers include Keith Kahn-Harris, Dara McGarry, Nick Jessup, Alex Romeo, Haresh Patel and Bridget Minamore.

Dan Kieran did the show in February 2017, and his genuine enthusiasm and encouragement helped us to see the potential within it. He's been a great advocate for the show and a real mentor to us over the years as well – and the subsequent publication of his *OneTrackMinds* story on his Medium page gave us the idea for this book. Thank you, Dan! (Kristian still owes you lunch.)

We really owe a huge debt of thanks to the marvellous Steve Chapman, whose long list of contacts and all-round delightfulness has led to us meeting so many brilliant people who have become contributors to the show. Steve also designed us a super-cool T-shirt and poster in support of this book, which helped us reach our funding target.

Special thanks to Carrie and David Grant, who've had us as a guest on their brilliant BBC London radio show on several occasions.

A huge thanks to Luke Wright for introducing us to so many of our brilliant storytellers over the years, including Jemima and Joe for our first nights. We've not yet managed to get Luke on to the show (although we've had a couple of near misses), but we'll get there one day.

Savannah James Bayly has introduced us to several guests who we've had on the show and have turned out to be brilliant. Thank you, Savannah.

And Rufus Wright has also opened up his extensive actorly Rolodex to help us build up our list of storytellers. You're a hero.

In 2018 we started doing our spin-off show, *Hidden Tracks*, which is kind of an open-mic night *OneTrackMinds*, where anyone with a story can sign up to take part. We owe a huge thanks to the first brave souls to pioneer that show – Janine Harouni, Nick Shakinovsky, Helen Fleming, Andrew Nolan, Rosa Dachtler, Nicholas Jessup, Dominic Fitch, Dara McGarry, Hannah Rodger, Harriet Allner, Cordi Walsh and Jess Nicks. And a special thanks to Harriet Allner for letting us use her office space for workshops, and for coming up with the name *Hidden Tracks* in the first place.

At the end of 2019 we did a very special show in collaboration with the brilliant community choir Camden Voices. That show came about thanks to the marvellous Isobel Pietsch, who had the idea of getting her choir to perform the songs chosen by our storytellers. She introduced us to choirmaster extraordinaire Ed Blunt, and thanks to the support of Jenny Barley at House of St Barnabas, we put on one of our most memorable shows. Thanks to Ed, to the storytellers on that night – Kate Keara Pelen, Ned Westaway and Laima Ulozaite – and to the Camden Voices themselves, Alex Wiseman, Lucy Knowles, Anna Wyatt, Amy Hall, Chloe Ravat, Lise Lovland, Harriet Crawford, Katy Kuhurt, James Rees, Seth Stromboli, Brendan Jacot, Ed John, Lawrence Walker, Tom James and Ugo Rosano.

We've often thought about ways of trying to expand *OneTrackMinds* to a wider audience and onto different platforms beyond the stage show. The first person to encourage us to explore the visual side of the show was the lovely Joe Marcus, who filmed one of our shows back in 2017 and spent a lot of time editing it together. He also chipped in with a very generous donation to this book. Thank you, Joe.

We also owe a huge thanks to Cameron Turnbull and Ben Cooper-Bland, who have filmed several of our shows since then, and always done so with great energy and enthusiasm. Thanks to Haresh Patel for all his advice and support when it comes to sound recording and for the insanely detailed work he did for the aforementioned choir show. Thanks too to William Walsh, who filmed that show for us (and who didn't punch Kristian after he mislaid his flight case full of extremely expensive camera lenses).

Adam and Kristian met while working at Agile Films – so thank you in particular to Myles Payne and David Staniland for accidentally introducing us, as well as for their support of this book. Agile have also loaned out their camera equipment on several occasions when we've recorded the show – huge thanks to Andy Eaton, Martin Fickling, Laurence Halstead, Aidan Brooks, Harry Chambers and the whole team for facilitating that.

We spent a significant chunk of 2019 working in the lovely red leatherette booths of the Soho Theatre Café and Bar, where we were made to feel immensely at home by the brilliant staff there, especially Caroline Regan, who always let us reserve our regular table and made the best lime and sodas.

Our brilliant team at Unbound have literally made this book what it is, and we're hugely grateful to them for their support. Particular thanks to our commissioning editor Katy Guest, to Georgia Odd and Cassie Waters for their help with our fundraising and to Alex Eccles, Miranda Ward and Hugh Davis for their help in editing the book.

Finally, to everyone who has ever bought a ticket to one of our shows (or indeed anyone who has been dragged along by a friend and not left at the interval), thank you so much for coming along and supporting our show. In particular, we must single out Georgina and Maria Poullais, Rhonda Rickman and Claire Paternoster, who have bought tickets to every single one of our shows at Wilton's Music Hall, and who've brought along many of their friends as well.

We're writing this at the end of February 2021, well over a year into the pandemic that has prevented us from doing our show in front of an audience for a painfully long time. This enforced absence from the MainStage at Wilton's Music Hall and festival stages across the country has made us so aware of just how much we miss you all, and how grateful we are to you for making *OneTrackMinds* so much fun.

We hope to see you all again in person very soon.

Kristian Brodie

Eternal and infinite thanks to my parents, Gun and Michael Brodie, who have always encouraged me in everything I've ever done. My dad's enthusiasm for the books, music and films that he loved opened up a whole world of stories and entertainment that I've revelled in ever since. My mum's passion for Barry Manilow had less of a role in shaping my cultural tastes, but her generosity and kindness helped shape me in other ways. I love you both very much.

My younger sister Kelly was the subject of the first *OneTrackMinds* story I wrote. It's not included in this book, but it was about how music brought us closer together as siblings and friends. Sharing songs and recommendations with her has been one of the great pleasures in my life, and even though she's now thousands of miles away in Melbourne with her awesome wife

Candeece and their gorgeous daughter Astrid, I'm so grateful for the relationship we have today. (Also, Kelly and Candeece came to one of our shows on the night before their wedding in July 2019.)

My older sister Ulrika has always been an inspiration to me too. One day I'll persuade you to come and tell your own story on the *OneTrackMinds* stage.

There are many brilliant things about being married to Zoe Jones (of whom more in a moment), but one of them is that she's one of seven children, and so, relatively late in my life, I've been gifted a whole new family of brothers and sisters – and a pair of new parents – all of whom have loved me and supported me as part of their (huge) family. Even though they're spread out across the world, from Escondido to Berlin, the collective Joneses have been a constant source of support throughout the life of *OneTrackMinds*. Thank you, Peter and Rebecca, Eowyn and David, Stasie, Julien and Christina, Myriam and Andy, Tessa and Toby. You guys are the best.

Glen Pierce was my 'tutor' at school – a sort of adviser/guidance counsellor, if you like – and I'm very glad that we're still in touch today. On the day I left school after my last A-level exam, I went to say goodbye to Glen. During our farewell he said something to me that I've never forgotten, and that made a big difference to how I interpreted the story of my life up to that point. I don't think I've ever thanked him properly for that, so now is a great opportunity.

With specific reference to my story, I'd like to thank my former colleagues at ContentFilm – in particular Jamie Carmichael, Harry White, Judith Baugin, Rebecca Berry, Graham Begg, Bea Neumann and Jed Benedict. I learned an awful lot during my three years working with you all, and I'm very grateful for everything you taught me (even if *Closing the Ring* was terrible).

Thanks to so many of my old friends who have been so supportive of the show over the years. In particular, John Babtie has dragged scores of people to the show since the beginning.

If we were to pay somebody to hype up *OneTrackMinds* on social media and via word of mouth, I'm sure they wouldn't do a better job than Chiara Ventura, who has been an absolute champion of our show since the beginning. She was also a great backstage assistant for a couple of shows in 2017, and she told a brilliant story on stage in 2018 as well. *Grazie molto!*

Another friend-turned-MainStage-storyteller is Claire Gordon Webster – thank you for all your encouragement, advice and support, and the many hours spent listening to me whinge about something or other over some sometimes questionable non-alcoholic beverages in south London.

And to James Bradley and Deborah Lilley, Afolabi Kuti, Nick Jessup, Izzy Pietsch, Joe Baker, Kara Durrett, Tom Goddard, Mia Collins and Ben O'Connell – thank you for your friendship and support.

Louis Shakinovsky – thank you for everything you have done for *OneTrackMinds* and our company VERYFINE. The advice, the support and mostly the belief in what Adam and I have been trying to do over the last few years has been absolutely priceless. You're a genuine hero.

Since February 2018, *OneTrackMinds* has become a more enjoyable part of my life, and that is down to one man. Adam Shakinovsky is, quite simply, the best human being I know, and I am so fortunate to have him as my partner on all things *OneTrackMinds* and VERYFINE. Your kindness, your energy and your positivity have powered us through so many trying times over the years (not least the process of getting this book funded), and without your spirit I'm certain that *OneTrackMinds* would have run into a proverbial wall some time ago. Your enthusiasm, your warmth and your sense of humour have made the journey we've taken nothing short of a pleasure. Here's to many many more years of *OneTrackMinds* and to many more exciting projects to come.

Finally, thanks to the two most special people in my life. My wife Zoe Jones is a truly amazing woman who helped me to redefine what really matters in life. Thank you for loving me – even when I'm not particularly loveable – and for supporting me in all that I do. And my daughter Malin, who showed me just how much love it is possible to feel for someone, and who inspires me every day to be the best person that I can be. You are the greatest.

Adam Shakinovsky

I was in my kitchen at home around Christmas 2017 when my old friend Kristian called me out of the blue. 'Shak, I wanted to see if you'd be one of the storytellers on *OneTrackMinds* on 15 February. Have a think. No pressure. I just thought you'd be really good.'

My stomach started doing cartwheels and the best kind of adrenaline started coursing through my veins (and hasn't properly stopped since).

At the time I didn't know the journey saying yes would take me on. So it seems fitting to start my personal acknowledgements with my partner in crime, Kristian. More on this to follow, but in the meantime...

In preparing that first story I want to thank my wife and best friend Elizabeth Jane. Multiplying joys and evaporating sorrow aside, you always make time to help me honestly and lovingly. Without your care of me and, in this case, suggestion that I speak with a GP, my story would be missing a happy ending – and I would be missing you.

My beloved Molly Grace. My story in this book ends where you began. We dance together to so many songs and share so many stories and myths, yet we are also bound together by this song in a way that you will perhaps only understand when you are old enough to read why. Also, I would like to thank you for insisting that £7 of your pocket money was to be the final pledge that made this book a reality. And I would also like to thank you for letting your brother Toby pay half in the end so he could share the glory.

My Toby William. You were not born when these events occurred, though you were by the time I stood on stage at Wilton's. While this story features your sister, the hopes and dreams that I have for being a father, and being here when I am needed most, apply every inch as much to you and your bouncing, leaping, generous-spirited, Pokémon-loving face.

I would like to thank my old friend Dominic Fitch, who came to my office in the middle of the day to help me – and gently suggested (100 per cent correctly) that the story that I should be telling was in fact not the one I had spent weeks preparing. Also, who heroically armed me with *awesome* workshop games before running my first *Hidden Tracks* session for storytellers.

Oliver Refson and Lilah Vandenburgh took time out of their gruelling writing/directing TV schedule to workshop my delivery so that it went from 'Well, that was a pleasantly told story' to something much more immediate, and significantly improved. Your talent and generosity have remained so constant – and up on my wall I still have your quote that I scribbled down on the night to stop me parroting lines: 'Go out there fully accepting the possibility of failure – anything else would be too defensively minded.' Thank you, Goose. Thank you, General. And thank you, Penny (RIP).

Another huge thanks goes to Helen Fleming. Not only has your professional support and steadfast friendship over these years been phenomenal, but you have always had my back. In addition to your many production duties, you always took time to listen and to support loads of our shows, at one of which we were lucky enough to hear your own incredible story.

So many of you all listened to, and helped better, each new draft of the story ahead of the night. So my endless thanks to:

Layf Shakur, for taking time in Bayswater to tell it to me straight and get me sharing rather than reading.

Paolo Principe Chianta. How many years have we known each other? How many of each other's books, plays, poems, etc. have we read? I do know that I rely on your talent to better mine, and this was no exception.

Dr Katie Hamilton, for allowing me to use this talk and my experience to help you educate mental-healthcare professionals. Our adventures are so rich with laughter and learning.

Alice Martin, for making me feel safe to try any and every idea out with you and know that I will get back warm and constructive feedback.

My wonderful siblings and family: Tania, Marc, Nicholas, Susan, Zsolt, Naomi, Matthew, Mercedes, Peter, Sue, Sam, Andrew and Alex. For listening to the drafts, for coming to the show and for everything else.

Emma Willis, Darragh Ooi, Hannah Rodger, Richard Cheesman-Prince, Jennifer Sheridan, Jill Worsley, Amber Millington, Laurence Halstead, Chris and Kika Dabbs. For being there when it matters most.

Rachel Gentile, for pointing out the comic nuances of rectal examination.

Barry Bassett, for letting me tell you the story in Metrobank in the middle of the day and crying in front of the teller.

Laura Ng, for taking a call and listening while probably set dressing King's Landing.

Max Myers, for coming to almost every show. For always inspiring me to tell better stories.

On the night itself I'd like to thank Andy Nyman, Cariad Lloyd and Bridget Minnamore, who, whether they knew it or not, made me feel as if I belonged in their company and put me fully at ease.

My friend Marianna Kulukundis also deserves a mention here. It was in part your encouragement that helped me take a leap from 'Well that was a lovely adventure' to 'I guess I'm in this for the long haul, then...'

Acknowledgement in focus should also go to my mother, Shirley. You yourself are the most evocative and transporting storyteller anyone could have the pleasure to meet. Plus you came out to watch the show and stayed well past your bedtime, even until the final 'Rage Against the Machine Track' finished the show.

Also to my father, Louis. For your support, guidance and love. Your life is rich with so many adventures that have, and still do, generate so many incredible stories.

Zoe Jones, thank you for always making me welcome in Maynard Road after (and sometimes before) a show.

Now, a call-back acknowledgement. Since that first appearance on the *OTM* MainStage back in 2018, Kristian has asked me back to tell the story again on a number of occasions. Each time was a thrill and a shining memory.

Not only did he found *OTM*, but indeed founded my role in it as his partner, encouraging me to co-host (and host), lead workshops and run show after show together. We've heard so many mind-blowing stories, and had so many discussions about each one, trying to work out its individual magic.

OneTrackMinds has brought with it so much joy and learning. I have met more wonderfully generous and talented people in three years than I could ever have foreseen. And it all happened because he picked up the phone and said, 'Hey, Shak...'

Finally, I would like to express profound thanks to the NHS. In particular the staff at Chelsea and Westminster, Kensington Park Medical Centre, Dr Simon Moore, Packers Surgery, Dr Sahar Hassan, and now St Peter's. While my story captures the confusion I experienced upon diagnosis, it does not detail the immense care, skill and support that has kept me healthy and happy for nearly a decade and counting. Thank you. (And also for the rectal probe.)

Unbound is the world's first crowdfunding publisher, established in 2011.

We believe that wonderful things can happen when you clear a path for people who share a passion. That's why we've built a platform that brings together readers and authors to crowdfund books they believe in – and give fresh ideas that don't fit the traditional mould the chance they deserve.

This book is in your hands because readers made it possible. Everyone who pledged their support is listed below. Join them by visiting unbound.com and supporting a book today.

Jed Benedict

Paul Benedyk

Mark Bennett

Nicky & Dan Bentham

Amanda Blainey

Morven Bolam

James Bolton

Joe Bond & Emily Benbow

Natalie Booroff

Abigale Borsberry

Daniel Bowden

Julia Bowden

James Bradley

Fiona Brands

Andy Brereton

Kelly Brodie

Michael Brodie

Ralph Brodie

Malin Brodie-Jones

Lizzie Brown

Brian Browne

Martin Bryant

Vena Bucholtz

Johnny Burns

Luis Carreola

Richard Cheesman-Prince

Paolo Chianta

Catriona Child

Juan Christian

Lauren Clark

Marie Cloux

Martin Colyer

Andrew Conlan

Andrea Cook

Jude Cook

Harry Cooke

Daniel-Konrad Cooper

Bernie Corbett

Roger Cordjohn

Sarah Cripps

Pippa Cross

Fiona Crowle

Nicole Croxford

Jordan Crute

Sam Cryer

Kevin Cullinan

Chris Dabbs

Andrew Dakers

Alexander Darby

Gareth Davies

Gareth Davies

Matt Davies

Sarah Dawson

Igor Degtiarev

Imogen Deller-Evans

Andrew Demianyk

Louisa Dent

Peter Dodds

Craig Donaghy

Kara Durrett

Andy Eaton

Kathryn Edwards

Simon Edwards

Anthony Eggington

Humphrey Elles-Hill

Katie Elliott

Rosie Elliott

Heath Ellis

Peter Emery

Kenny Endlich

Pauline Eyre

Scott Fawcett

Anne Marie Fay

Chris Ferguson

Laura Ferguson

Patric ffrench Devitt

Martin Fickling

Kath Fielder

Will Fihn Ramsay

Patrick Fischer

Dominic Fitch

Em Fleming

Garrie Fletcher

Zoe Flower

Billy Flynn Johnson

Clare Fowler

Lisa Fox

Anthony Freinberg

Josephine Gallagher

Rufus Gerrard-Wright

Ellie Gibbons

Lyn Gibson

Jon Gilbert-Farrell

Charlie Gladstone

Ros Godber

Tom Goddard

Michael Goodridge

Claire Gordon-Webster

Rae Gould

Sam Gover & Robin Sager

Ed Gowan

Nick Gray

Jono Green

Nicholas Greene

Georgia Greer

Katy Guest

Ashish Gupta

William H-S

Andrea Hadley-Johnson

Phil Hall

George Hamilton

Katie Hamilton

Irene Hannah

Jason Hares

Kate Harford

Maria Harrington

Pete Harris

Jonathan Harrison

Rachel Hazelwood

Richard Hein

C Held

Paul Henly

Myriam Hertzog

Nicole Hess-Waldron

Ryan Hewitt

Kate Higney

Rich Hill

Sean Hill

Daphnée Hocquard

Tom Hodgson

Kamilla Hodol

Cato Hoeben

Mark Holbrook

Diane Hollis

Rhys Houghton-Jones

Chris Howard

Chris Hulbert

Jane Hyndman

Laura Jackson

Savannah James-Bayly

David Jamison

Nicholas Jessup

Janice Johnson

Laurel Johnson

Gabrielle Jones

Kate Jones

Rebecca Jones

Tobias Jones

Zoe Jones

Emilie Jouffroy

Caroline Joyce

Sam Judah

Keith Kahn-Harris

Oliver Kassman

Brid Keane

David Keeley

Hilary Kemp

Dan Kieran

Robert Killheffer

Anna Kolber

Rob Kraitt

Leander Kreltszheim

Karen Krizanovich

Marianna Kulukundis

Afolabi Kuti

Anna Lahert

Ben Lambert

Ali Larkin

Andrew Lavelle

Joanne Lawlor

Stefano Lazzaro

Huy Le

Andy Lear

Andrew Lees

Elizabeth Lenherr

Tim LeRoy

Sophie Lerway

Penny Lewis

Ben Lithman

Susie Lithman-Romeo

Aaron Lobb

Heidi Logie

Kari Long

Maisie Lynch

Rob MacAndrew

Gabrielle Mahdesian

Salvador Maldonado
John Manning
Joe Marcus
Paul Marino
Jethro Marks
Alice Martin
Rebecca McCormick
Peter McCowie
Katrina McCrudden
Dara McGarry
Marie McGinley
Andrew McGrouther
M J McMahon
Toby McMillan
Stuart McPhee
Barbara Joan Meier
Ineke Meijer
Bertie Meyer
Christos Michaels
Jacob Migicovsky
Amber Millington
Caroline Milsom
John Mitchinson
Anna Mohr-Pietsch
Emily Morgan
James Morgan
Cathleen Morrin
Stuart Morrow
Victoria Mottershead
Blair Mowat
Joerg Mueller-Kindt

Carlos Munoz
Gus and Julie Murray
Joe Myers
Max Myers
Kath Nagle
Carlo Navato
Fleur Neale
Aadel Nodeh Farahani
Diana Nowacka
Claire Oakley
Liam OConnor
Maggie Odonohoe
Darragh Ooi
Peter Orr
Angela Osborne
Luke Palmer
Eduardo Panizzo
Nick Parker
Steven Parker
Hannah Patterson
Myles Payne
Robert Peck
Ken Petrie
Glen Pierce
Isobel Pietsch
Jon Plant
Philip Podmore
Justin Pollard
Georgina Poullais
Maria Poullais
Robert Poynton

Michelle Prince

Kirsten Proctor

David Prosser

Tom Raffe

Gwen Rahardja

Phil Ratcliffe

Tessa Reed

Rhonda Rickwood

Ellie Rocks

Hannah Rodger

Alex Romeo

Pippa Russell

Vanessa Sammut

Jemma Sawyer

Ian Scorer

Simon Scott

Jeff Seamster

Elizabeth Shakinovsky

Marc Shakinovsky

Molly Shakinovsky

Tania Shakinovsky

Toby Shakinovsky

Alison Shaw

Kate Shaw

Mark Shayler

Robert Shearman

David Sheldon

Jennifer Sheridan

Samuel Shorr

Jo Ellen Shumway

John Sigmund

James Sills

Jenna Simes

Alexia Singh

Flora Smith

Karen Smith

Matt Smith

Kura Solon

Marcia Sousa

Catherine Spanswick

Ellie Spruell

@stevexoh

Paul Stevens

Eowyn Stoddard

Kate Stonehill

Jon Stones

Roger Sumner

Simone Talfourd

Becky Tanner-Rolf

Jack Tarling

William Teddy

Maggi Testot-Newick

Dominic Thompson

Amanda Thomson

Georgina Thomson

Dean Threadgold

Piers Torday

Mark Towers

Martin Trotter

Natalie Trotter-King

Eleanor Tweddell

Isabella Valentini

Tony Vanderheyden

Chiara Ventura

Eduardo Vidal

Ian Walker a.k.a. "Dr. Soul"

Peter Ware

Rob Watson

Bethan Way

Emma Webb

Barbara Wheatley

Ben Whitehouse

Karl Wickens

Louise Wilkin

Susan Wilkins

Mark Williams

Ludwig Wolf

Peter Wood

Tom Wood

Paul Woodward

Amy Wright

Charlie Wuppermann

Jac Wynn